# THE RESILIENCE ROADMAP

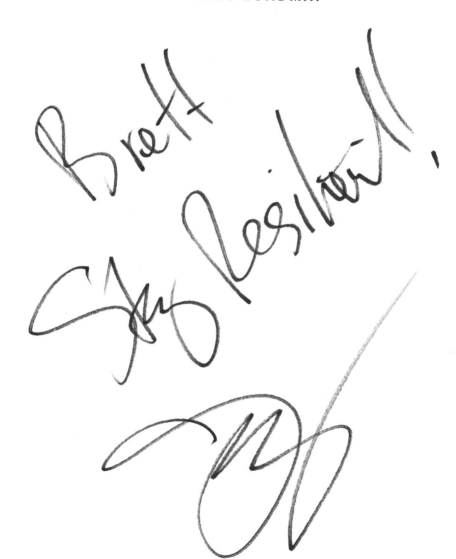

Brett

Stay Resilient!

# THE

# RESILIENCE

# ROAD MAP

//DANNY MOREL//

AUTHOR · COACH
HOST · TRAINER

A GUIDE TO BUILDING
YOUR IDEAL BUSINESS

THE RESILIENCE ROADMAP

*A Guide to Building Your Ideal Business*

ISBN   978-1-61961-645-5 *Paperback*

   978-1-61961-646-2 *Ebook*

*To my wife, Claudia, who stood by me in our worst moments.*

*You are the most resilient person I know.*

*I love you.*

# CONTENTS

. . . . . . . .

# INTRODUCTION

## FROM HUMBLE BEGINNINGS

I learned to be resilient at age thirteen, after my parents divorced. I grew up in New York City, and, after my parents split up, I moved with my mom and siblings to Southern California. Real estate wouldn't enter the picture until much later, but I believe the seeds of my success as both an entrepreneur and sales coach were planted during the disruption of that cross-country move and the challenges that followed.

You have to be resilient when your old life is wiped away and your new life is a single-parent household with public assistance just to put food on the table. I was accustomed to private school and having both parents around, but I quickly learned that I was solely responsible for how my life would turn out. So I started working to live my ideal life someday—a life that would include financial security, not food scarcity and fear.

I didn't know at the time what my path to success would look like, but I realize now that resiliency was at the heart of my journey. Failure and setbacks would not slow me down as long as I kept my eyes focused on moving forward with every step.

Education was a challenge in a public school that was one of the worst in the state. Neighborhood crime was a fact of everyday life. I was outside playing baseball with my little brother one day when twenty SWAT officers raided an apartment across the street.

To imagine that someone from my neighborhood could make $1.5 million a year in commissions and live in a 6,000 square foot house by age twenty-seven was laughable. Success of that magnitude was unfathomable when a parent struggled just to put food on the table.

I'm living proof that dreams are only impossible until you make them possible.

I credit my mother, who was the picture of resiliency during my childhood. She instilled in me the same indomitable spirit. Watching her made me want more for my life. She was a young Hispanic woman, maybe four foot ten, when she moved us across the country without a driver's license. She hadn't yet attained U.S. citizenship.

She did it because she wanted a better life for her boys. I saw her sacrificing for us, and I wanted to give something back to her. So I took it upon myself, as soon as I could, to buy her a house. I was just twenty-one. I wanted to thank her for everything she'd done for us and prove to myself that I could break the cycle of poverty.

Everything that followed—my brokerage, financial security, the ability to help others through coaching, and even this book—began with the singular desire to buy a house for my mom. I consider it poetic justice that I would later make my living helping others find their dream homes.

I can recall living in that cramped apartment and watching *Beverly Hills 90210* and seeing those kids grow up with nice cars and beautiful homes. Even at my school, there were some who had it better. Rather than making me bitter about my situation, I saw their lives as proof that there was more out there for my family and me. If other people could have it, I would find out what I had to do to have it too.

## THE KEY THAT UNLOCKED THE DOOR

Real estate ended up being the key that unlocked the door for me. I stumbled into the profession quite by accident. I had just graduated high school and had this goal of getting us a house. At the time, I was a full-time college student, ran a tortilla delivery business, and was working as a recruiter for a local job corps. I had started to save up a little bit of money to make my goal a reality and actually buy a house.

One weekend, when I was working a job fair, I saw a real estate agent working across the way from me. He had pictures of houses at his stand, and here I was working to buy a house, so naturally I went across the room and spoke to him.

The guy seemed like he did OK in life, which got me thinking about the business side of real estate. At the time, I was just young and hungry for any opportunity, so I asked him a question that started me down this road. I'll never forget it. I was already working six days a week, but I asked him, "Is there any money in real estate?" He told me there was. I said, "Tell you what, I'll work for you for free on Sundays if you'll just teach me the business."

He agreed, and that next Sunday I showed up to his house at four in the morning. My job was to set up his booth at a swap meet. The agent told me, "If you can get me five leads, this will be worth my time." People would walk by and look at pictures of the same homes that caught my attention, and I'd answer any questions they asked.

I got him twenty-five leads that day. That's when I knew I had a knack for sales.

What spurred me to get my real estate license happened a few months later. I was at another swap meet when those same clients I'd originally scouted came by and complained about their loan or the house they'd bought. They were basically calling me a crook! I explained that all I'd done was take their contact information and pass it on to the agent.

I was defensive and crestfallen at how frustrated these people were. Their slice of the American dream had an asterisk next to it. I was forced to examine the unfulfilled promise in their situations, and this motivated me to get my license. I knew there was wrongdoing in how this guy handled his business and I wanted to fix that.

## WEATHERING THE STORMS OF LIFE

As I began to have success in real estate, a funny thing happened. I realized the childhood I was trying to escape, and all the adversity my family endured, factored into my success.

When my dad stepped out of our lives, I no longer had an option. People with options have a safety net, a plan B, a way out. Those options keep them from sacrificing at the level that success requires. People who don't have options sink or swim on their own. When your father leaves, and you're the oldest, it's up to you. Either you're going to make it happen or your family will suffer. That was my motivation then and now.

I see it today with the people I coach. I'll teach them every technique that's led to my repeated success, and they can't grasp it or get the same kind of results. Typically, when I dig deep enough, I find out the problem is that they have other options. They have that escape hatch. There's rental income, income from the military, or retirement money coming in that reduces their incentive to fight for their dreams.

When I started out in business, I drew on the fact that I was on my own. If I wanted to do great things in my life, I had to make it happen, or it wasn't going to happen at all. It was as simple as that.

My mom showed her resilience again, later, when she battled cancer. Not once during those five years did she tell me she was sad or in pain. She had a deep faith that kept her positive and fighting until the very end.

Others we knew who were also ill passed away within five or six months. Mom outlasted them all and passed that faith and endurance on to us.

## IT ALL CAME CRASHING DOWN

Tough times found me again in 2008 when the market crashed. A lot of people I knew in business went through it but weren't as affected as I was. Then again, they didn't go as big as I did when I started my own coaching business. I took a huge leap of faith, and when the market tanked, I fell hard. I didn't have enough money invested or saved, and for that I take full responsibility. You have to own up to your mistakes and grow from them.

When it happened, I was running my coaching company, and we had about 500 Realtors who were paying us monthly to coach and motivate them to be better at sales. Within a six-month period, we lost 60 percent of our clients, as mortgage offices and real estate offices shut down overnight. It got so bad that I was forced to leave the industry.

It was another drastic change in my life. In two years, I'd gone from the twenty-seven-year-old making over a million dollars a year and living in a custom-built home, to the guy with a wife and two kids who eventually had to move in with his mom. That's how bad it got. I was making $1,200 a month doing multilevel marketing and living with my wife and kids in one bedroom.

I'll never forget the day that really woke me up. It was 105 degrees outside, and our air conditioner broke. I couldn't afford to get it fixed. I want you to picture this scenario and imagine the guilt I felt. I had to sit the kids in an ice chest with water just to cool them off. I took a picture and still have it to this day. The kids are smiling in the picture because they were babies who didn't know any different. They thought it was fun.

For me, that moment was the breaking point. I knew I was meant for more than this, which meant it was time for me to do something.

## A PEOPLE-CENTERED APPROACH

That breaking point sparked my motivation to get back to basics. I had to put my ego aside for a little bit and go back to selling real estate, which was something I had moved on from when I stepped into the coaching world. But it's what I had to do to better my family.

As I got my feet wet selling real estate again, I began to envision the next brokerage I wanted to open. The first thing I did was recognize that there was room for disruption in the industry. Real estate, for the most part, is a broken industry. There's no value in the relationship between a broker and an agent. My belief was validated when my coaching company signed up 500 agents in the first year. Our success showed the need in our industry for the leadership we offered.

One thing all successful businesses have in common when they start is that there's something unique about them. They bring something to the party that nobody else is bringing. My value proposition was very clear: my new business would be all about my people.

I committed to following the golden rule of helping enough people get what they want, because I knew that meant I'd be taken care of. I did that on a large scale and focused on helping my people become better at sales. Combining the Golden Rule and sales training has made us an Inc. 500 company that will do a billion dollars in sales this year.

In rising from the ashes with my new brokerage, Intero Real Estate Services, I saw that funny thing happening again, where my personal trajectory was informing the philosophy I shared with clients. I can't stand the thought of people all around me settling for a life of mediocrity. I came from a life of poverty and being stuck at that level always bugged me. I thought to myself, "This is America. There are a lot of people doing amazing things and I know I can do amazing things, as well." That really shaped my philosophy.

Now everything I do focuses on helping others achieve their own success. Life is more fun when everybody's doing great together. As an agent just starting out, I made sure to stay hungry by surrounding myself with people who were doing much better than I was. Now as a broker, I've added over 400 real estate salespeople to my team who can motivate each other in the same way. We're a community helping each other to do better than we could do by ourselves.

My motivation for writing this book was to reach more people and show them what's possible. Our company has been successful because we keep people and purpose ahead of money. That was the mission from day one. Now, as a businessman, do I look at our profit and loss numbers? Absolutely. But am I thinking I need to make more money? Never. I'm focused on growing the company so we can help more people. That's our philosophy.

## A WINNING FORMULA

Even if you're not in real estate, this bedrock philosophy still applies to you.

Let me use an example to show you what I mean. If you're a restaurateur who's focused strictly on profit, you'll buy cheap ingredients and spend next to nothing decorating your restaurant just to save a buck. But by focusing solely on the bottom line, you've lost sight of the value you're delivering to the customer. You're not putting yourself in the shoes of the people who come to your restaurant seeking flavorful food, comfortable furniture, and a nice ambience.

Same thing if you're hosting a friend at your house. If you want to be a good host, you'll cook a nice meal and get a bottle of wine. That's putting your guest first. This mindset applies to any business in any industry. Put people and purpose first and profit will follow.

At the core of this philosophy is resiliency. When you're not focused on money, there are times when you'll look at your bank account or profit and loss reports and cringe. But you can rest assured that success will come, because you're committed to putting people and purpose first. Resiliency is born out of this determination to fulfill your vision.

A winning spirit makes it easier to remain committed. A lot of people have a hard time saying they want to win, because they don't want to come off as arrogant. Every student wants to get a good grade, right? Every performer wants to get a standing ovation. Nobody wants to do anything poorly or wakes up and says, "I'm going to suck at life today."

Don't be afraid to admit your desire to accomplish great things. If you don't embrace that winning spirit, the bumps and bruises you'll experience during your journey will knock you back and you'll get emotional, causing you to quit before your potential is fulfilled.

I know you're not a quitter. You're like me—too resilient to throw in the towel. You believe, like I did growing up in that tiny apartment, that you're destined for greatness. You see all the thrilling possibilities of your life, and now you're figuring out how to get there.

This book will help you get where you want to go by first enhancing your mind-set. Not only that, we're going to enhance your belief system, your possibility thinking, and learn how to exercise what I call your "faith muscle." To show you why mind-set enhancement is critical, let me tell you a little about my brokerage, Intero Real Estate in Rancho Cucamonga, California.

At the time I'm writing this, in early 2017, we have a chance to finish the year as the number one real estate brokerage in Southern California. In terms of closed transactions in our multiple listing service (MLS), we're ranked first right now. The crazy part is that we're doing this with 120 fewer agents than the other top-ranked companies. How is that possible?

It's because our message touches the lives of those who work here and causes them to enhance their mind-sets. We're taking people at X and showing them how to get to Y and Z. That's what you can expect to take away from this book. If you're success-minded and want to do something amazing in life, or you have an idea but don't know how to get it out, or you're dealing with hard times and you're afraid, this book will show you, step by step, how to conquer those obstacles and make your idea a reality.

There have been times in my life when I've had to persevere, and I'm going to show you how to leverage those tough times. To be honest, I grow the most during tough times, because that's when I have my back up against the wall. There's absolutely no choice but to step up or get out of the game, and I have to make it happen.

Part of the winning formula is understanding that tough times have a lot to do with your perspective. When I was down and out after the market crash, I was hurt. I was depressed. We all get to the point sometimes where we'll say, "Well, things can't get any worse." People with a changed mind-set will look at rock bottom and say to themselves, "I might as well push forward, because the only way I can go from here is up."

We're also going to address low emotional maturity. Most business owners aren't born entrepreneurs, but were instead employees who had an idea to start their own business. As we all know, there's a lot of risk in that process. With that risk comes doubt, and with that doubt comes fear.

Then all it takes is one little thing going wrong—a bad day in sales or somebody stealing from you—to validate that fear and doubt and worry. That's when business owners with low emotional maturity create a story so negative it engulfs everything they think about.

I'll show you how to address these feelings and work past them. We'll examine how fear comes not from ourselves, but rather from our egos. Once you can understand that distinction, you'll be able to separate from your anxiety and deal with it in a positive way. If this sounds intimidating, don't worry! We're going to give you the tools to be able to handle that.

I also want to address this myth that being successful means working longer and harder hours. That's only true in the beginning. As with any endeavor, you have to pay the price when you start in business, because you have very little leverage.

The challenge of an entrepreneur is gaining leverage, and I think there are two ways of doing that: through other people and through cash. I started our company with $2,000 in my pocket. As a matter of fact, I never raised capital for any of the companies I started. I just had a vision, put together a plan of action, and followed the steps I'm going to teach you in this book.

Everything eventually came to fruition, but only after working the long hours that were required to get the job done. After a couple of years, your business should start to produce enough that you can leverage yourself through things like marketing, advertising, and hiring employees. Just like a baby has to learn how to crawl before it can walk, business owners have to first work longer and harder before they can work less and produce more.

My strategies will make that strenuous start-up period feel less daunting.

## SEVEN PRINCIPLES OF RESILIENCY

As you've already seen, resiliency and overcoming adversity are at the core of my philosophy of life and success. It's why I wrote this book. I want to show you the way I learned, which is why I developed what I call the "seven principles of resiliency." Each of the following chapters will focus on one of these seven principles.

- Principle One: Live by Faith, Not Fear
- Principle Two: Decide What You Want
- Principle Three: Make a Plan
- Principle Four: Take Massive, Inspired Action
- Principle Five: Track Your Numbers
- Principle Six: Make Adjustments Based on the Numbers
- Principle Seven: Don't Be Attached to the Outcome

These principles will help you align your heart and soul, and break down your fears to see what's possible. Once that happens, you'll be a human being who has grown to capacity, and we can move on to action steps meant to help you build a successful business. But first, we have to build a successful mind. That's very important.

If you're looking for a foolproof way to achieve success, I believe my seven principles will help you achieve whatever it is you're trying to accomplish. My confidence stems from the fact that rather than selling you some get-rich-quick scheme that's doomed to fail, I'm helping shape you into a forward-thinking person who chews up problems and spits out solutions. It doesn't matter if you're trying to start a business with zero capital or countless investor dollars in the bank.

I've never started anything with deep pockets backing me up. Intero Real Estate is the best example I can give you of how to actualize a vision you have for your life. We're talking about a business I started with $2,000, and we'll do $36 million in revenue and are shooting for over a billion dollars in sales this year. My team and I got there by following the principles I'm going to teach in this book.

You don't need an MBA to understand these principles. They're not complicated, but rather are commonsense ideas most people just haven't been exposed to yet.

I built this book around resiliency because nobody is immune to adversity. Any notion I had of that false reality went away the moment I moved my family into a bedroom in my mom's house. Life happens. We're always going to run across problems, whether in business or at home.

The key difference with people who produce at a high level is that they're wired in a way to deal with the daily circumstances that are desperately trying to knock them off track. This book will reveal the secrets of how to become undaunted by adversity.

I want to end on an uplifting note, and to do that I'm going to include some words I have framed in my office. They are the words that I wrote down when I first opened our company:

*We are a place of change, we are a place of breakthroughs, we are a place of growth.*

That's what this book is all about: change, breakthroughs, and growth. We're going to take those of you who can't see and help you see big. When you start to see big, you start to believe in possibilities. When you start to believe in possibilities, you'll begin to take inspired actions. Those actions will lead you into the life you were destined to live, and you'll start to believe you can accomplish anything you want to do. That's when you'll change the world.

I'm ready to go. Are you?

Good. Let's get started.

*Principle One*

# LIVE BY FAITH, NOT FEAR

. . . . . . . .

I have never encountered the kind of shame I felt after the market crash of 2008. As someone who grew up working hard for every dollar I earned, I was devastated to have it all stripped away so quickly. I agonized over where I went wrong and how I might have done things differently and been more prepared. "This is all my fault," I told myself, and it was. Accepting responsibility for what happens in your life is fundamental to success.

The first gut punch was moving from our home, which I had fought so hard to build, into a rental home that was half the size. My income kept dwindling to the point that we had to start selling TVs, suits, watches—essentially liquidating everything just to pay the bills and make rent.

The punches weren't done coming. Eventually we could no longer afford rent and had to move in with my mother. Imagine being a provider for your family and telling the people you love that we have to move again because daddy can't pay the rent. Picture the looks on your family's faces as you deliver that news to them, and you can understand my heartbreak.

My guilt also stemmed from the fact that, as a young single man, I did some amazing things financially. Now, as a married man with two children, I couldn't put two pennies together.

Looking back at that experience, I think it was meant to teach me humility. It was something that I had to taste, something I had to experience. I think you need humility if you're going to do anything great in this world. Humility helps you relate to people when they're going through their breakdowns. Even though it was painful, that was a very big step for me.

My failure also showed me the power of fear-based thinking. We attract and become whatever it is we think about, so the more you think in terms of fear, the more you attract situations, people, and circumstances that validate your fears. The more you think and live by faith, the more you attract people, circumstances, and situations that validate that faith.

I spent about a year and a half living in fear when the market crashed. When things started getting bad, I feared we would lose our house. After we lost the house, I worried we wouldn't be able to afford groceries or rent. Once we moved in with my mom, I wondered if things could get any worse, and that became the new source of my terror. Fear is a dark, bottomless pit filled with anxiety and worry that will swallow you whole the moment you take that leap.

The challenge is that it's easy to succumb to our fears. I walked right into my deepest and darkest nightmares and, as a result, my fears became my reality. I can remember lying in bed not wanting to get up and attempt anything. I didn't know which direction to go.

Hitting rock bottom made me realize you can't live in faith and also live in fear. You've got to choose one. That realization was the first step of getting our family out of that mess. It was the beginning of my ability to see what was possible for the company I wanted to open and how that would allow me to take better care of my family. That's when I finally stepped into faith.

## EMBRACING FAITH-BASED THINKING

You strengthen your faith through a process I like to call "building your faith muscle." If you can picture it, I'm doing a bicep curl right now. You might laugh, but that's what we're talking about!

Building your faith muscle is the same as building a great physique, in that neither happens overnight. You have to be consistent with both processes and be accountable. If you want a great physique, you have to get out of bed and go to the gym. It's the same thing with living in faith. If you don't consistently exercise faith, your faith muscle will atrophy.

Fear-based thinking can cripple your ability to do your job well. Let's say I'm a salesperson and I have to pick up the phone to make a sales call. If I have fear-based thinking, the thought of being rejected on that call is going to terrify me.

If I'm a public speaker who makes his living in front of people and I'm trapped in fear-based thinking, I'll struggle to effectively communicate my message to the audience. Because I'm allowing fear to dominate my thinking, I'm inevitably going to attract those situations and people that keep me buried in my fearful thinking.

If you're struggling with fear right now, you probably want to know how to shed that fear and embrace faith-based thinking. The first thing you've got to do is understand where you are in life. If you don't understand where you are, then you'll never know the steps to take to fix it.

Let's return to our hypothetical salesperson example. If I'm afraid of picking up that phone, I can start by committing to call just five people. Once I make those five calls, I'll assess my fear based on the reality of what happened during those conversations. Maybe I got one jerk on the phone, but I had four positive conversations.

"That wasn't so bad," I say to myself.

With that result in mind, I come in tomorrow and talk to ten people. Out of the ten, maybe one or two are nut jobs or really mean. But then you've got five or six that aren't that bad, and you have one or two really good conversations. As you start to see the reality of your situation, and that truth begins to wash away the fear you felt, you're building your faith muscle. Again, your fear won't disappear overnight. But as that faith muscle grows stronger through repeated exercise, your fear will shrink at the same rate.

To break through fear and start living in faith, you have to accept full responsibility for your life and how you handle those unexpected curveballs. Fear is based on the unknown and a lack of control. You will liberate yourself the day you realize that the only thing you can always control in life is the way you react. Once you realize that, you can begin to react positively instead of negatively, and you can grow from every situation. For those situations where you have no control, choose to exercise your faith muscle.

When something bad that's within your control happens, accept responsibility, and exercise your faith muscle all the same. You will come out the other side a better person.

Still, there are times when you're going to be afraid. Humans are just hardwired to have that reaction when confronting certain situations. If you're guilty of this like I was after the market crash, don't beat yourself up. We're not learning to avoid fear, we're learning to fight through it. Those who've enjoyed success have learned to master the conversation inside their head when their fear is ramping up. It's a process of growth, and there's no way around it if you really want to grow into something special.

Reliving the story of what happened when the market crashed is tough for me, because I'm a very positive and forward-thinking person. But at that time, I believe God needed to strip my ego and pride away so that I could grow and become who I am today.

Now, not only do I lead more than 400 salespeople and staff members at my company, but I'm also helping a lot of people through my podcasts and this book.

That experience made it so that I can genuinely connect with people, because I know what they're going through. I can look them in the eye and say, "It's OK. I've gone through it as well. Here's what I did to get out of it." That time of fear was transformational for me.

## FAITH GIVES YOU BETTER VISION

Now let's examine the flip side of fear. What do I mean by faith in this context? I see faith as being able to believe in a greater possibility, to have an idea and not focus on the roadblocks to realizing it.

When you're faith-based, you see possibilities, and you see answers. If you're fear-based, you see a brick wall. When the time comes to make a choice, faith propels you into the unknown, and fear wraps you in its ugly claws and pulls you away from your greater possibility.

Let me give you another example. Let's say I have an idea to open a restaurant. For the last ten years, everyone who comes to my house says my food is delicious. I know that my recipes are amazing, and I also have a knack for entertaining.

What I don't know is a lot about the restaurant business, which I could let hold me back. So many people who know they're onto something special let fear of the unknown hold them back. It's tragic. What they don't understand, especially with the resources available to us now, is that you can learn anything you want and apply it right away.

When you're living in faith, you use your reality to validate your dreams. I don't mean that to sound like you're delusional. If the hypothetical me who wanted to open a restaurant burned everything I cooked and hated having people over for dinner, I should avoid that particular business venture. But when everybody who comes to my house can't stop praising my food, I should use that reassurance to propel me forward. I might not know about the business side of running a restaurant, but I have enough faith in myself to know I can pull this off.

That's when you start confronting the questions that every entrepreneur faces: *How do I make this happen? What if we don't have the money to pay the bills this month? Where can I get the upfront cash to lease the building? How will I get the word out once we open our doors?*

Some entrepreneurs give up as soon as they confront these questions. But when you're living in faith, you answer any question with a solution. You're always thinking in possibilities.

## THE FORCES THAT SHAPE OUR FAITH

There are outside forces that influence your ability to live by faith that I call the ego and the spirit. The ego is inside us for one purpose and that is to keep us safe. It's there to keep us from ever being let down, experiencing failure, or feeling pain.

The ego shows up in a lot of different ways. You go to make a phone call, and the ego tells you small things like, "What happens if they don't like you?" or "What happens if they hang up on you?" You go to make a big presentation and are about to speak in front of a bunch of people, and the ego reminds you of something that happened to you when you were a small child that caused you to feel embarrassment.

You think of a business idea and the optimistic part of you says, "I could really pull this off," but the ego chimes in and says, "Look around you. You live in a crummy apartment with bills piled up on the table. Let's get real here. That idea will never happen."

The ego is there to keep us safe, but the problem is that nothing great happens from being safe. The only great things that happen in this world happen to people who learn how to tap into their spirit, which exists opposite the ego. When you're about to pick up the phone and call a prospect, the spirit says, "I know there's a potential prospect out there, so I'm going to keep moving forward until I find them."

The spirit has this response to your business idea: "I know I don't have all the resources yet, but I will get them, and everything will work out fantastic."

The spirit reminds you of the victories in your life, and the ego reminds you of the failures. The spirit pushes you into greatness and helps you believe that anything is possible. You move forward when you listen to the spirit and go backward when you listen to your ego. There is no standing still.

For the burgeoning restaurateur, the ego is the one asking how you'll raise the money to open a restaurant and reminding you of all the times you burned your food. Meanwhile, the spirit reminds you that everyone loves your food. The ego manipulates your worry. That's the difference between the ego and the spirit.

Along those same lines, I believe our inner world creates our outer world. This is the second outside influence that compels you to live by either faith or fear. Think about everything you have in your life right now. Your finances, relationships, health, even the clothes you wear are created in the outer world because of the thoughts and emotions in your inner world.

I'll give you an example. I only wear custom suits, but before I explain why, I want to discuss how our standards in life affect the quality of our lives. More specifically, the better you feel on a day-to-day basis, the more you'll be able to help other people.

Something as simple as the water you buy and where you buy it can impact how you feel on a daily basis. When I go buy a gallon of water at the local grocery store, they might have one option for alkaline water, which is a big deal to me. I love alkaline water because it helps hydrate my body, so instead of shopping at the grocery, I'll go to a farmer's market or a supermarket like Whole Foods, where they'll have a dozen different alkaline-water options. I know I'll feel better when I drink alkaline water, so instead of settling for limited options at the grocery, I make the extra effort to get what I need.

I've set a similar standard when it comes to wearing custom suits. If you buy a suit off the rack at Macy's or Nordstrom, you'll be out of pocket $400 for a good one. You can get a good custom suit with half decent material for about $700. We're talking about an extra $300 for something that is made specifically for you. A custom suit makes you look sharper and, more than anything, reinforces a strong self-belief, because you invested extra money in yourself, which is something most people don't do.

When I walk into a presentation and feel incredible because my suit fits just the way I like, my energy is better and therefore my chances of nailing the presentation are better. To grow my business, I have to feel amazing about myself, my potential, and my possibilities all day. Custom suits, like alkaline water, help me feel better, and the better I feel about myself inside, the better my outer world will become.

It's the same for any business owner, especially new ones. If they're constantly worrying about paying the rent, guess what happens? All of a sudden, they can't pay the rent. But if they're focused on how their product or service can impact other people, compassion will be created inside of them, they'll attract better customers, and their business will flourish.

I did the same thing with my wife. Before I was married, I wrote down in detail who I wanted my wife to be—her characteristics, her personality, everything about her. I wasn't going to settle for anything but the best. I wrote this in my journal on October 1, 2004.

I met my wife, Claudia, on October 1, 2005. Years later, when I finally looked at the book, I hopped out of bed and I yelled to my wife, "Babe, when did we meet? What was the date?" She said October 1, 2005. I was floored.

During our marriage, I've seen divorces left and right. I've never had to worry, because I know Claudia is resilient and holds true to the vows we took. If you ask me why I believe your inner world creates your outer world, all I need is to think back to the day I used my thoughts to find Claudia.

## PRACTICING FAITH EVERY DAY

Now that you understand the difference between fear- and faith-based thinking, between ego and spirit, and how the inner world creates the outer world, it's time to start living by faith every day.

Here are some actual activities you can do to begin that process.

1. **Make a list of five things you're grateful for in your life.** Focusing on the bad stuff is going to knock you off course, so look instead at the good things that make you feel inspired and motivated. When I think about my kids and envision their smiling faces, I can't help but smile. I feel thankful that God blessed me with them.

2. **Put on the biggest smile you can during your morning shower.** As you're smiling, think for a minute about what makes you happy, everything you want to accomplish, and all those things you're grateful for in life. (Use the list you just made!)

3. **Write out your goals on a sheet of paper.** Every day I write out my intentions for the current year. It doesn't matter if the events happen that year or not. Just by writing them down, I am more likely to achieve them. Why? Because I'm taking a part of my inner world—my goals—and using it to shape my outer world.

Those are some key activities that will help you begin to live by faith. Another thing I would recommend, although this one can be more difficult, is surrounding yourself with like-minded people. This is critical.

When you're committed to pursuing a greater possibility for your life, you must be aware that there are people out there who will say you're crazy. They'll give you every reason why you shouldn't attempt what you want to attempt. Little by little, you must eliminate these negative influences in your life and begin to associate yourself with positive individuals.

When I was younger, I had a roommate who was pretty messy, and the problem was that I'm not a messy person.

In fact, I'm borderline OCD. I like things organized and in their proper place. But little by little, this roommate wore me down. Things that used to bother me stopped bothering me. I gave up, gave in, and started to become more like that roommate.

Shoes would be out of the closet and scattered around the living room. I didn't care. Dirty dishes didn't bother me at all. My dedication to keeping a clean home started to dwindle because of this person I decided to associate myself with.

I think we do this all the time. Some people we surround ourselves with can't see past their current circumstances, so when you have goals, aspirations, and dreams, those people try to knock you down. They try to pull you backward and keep you from reaching for your dreams. These people aren't evil, just envious of your ambition to achieve greatness. It makes them feel bad about where they are in life, so they try to bring you down to their level.

You have to take a good, hard look at people like this in your life. Here's how you do that: Grab a piece of paper and draw a line down the middle. On the left side, write *Good*, and on the right side, write *Bad*. Now put the people in your life into the correct columns on that paper. Not good or bad people, just good or bad influences, those people who encourage you or hold you back.

I wrote that list when I was eighteen years old. After being honest with myself, I ended up putting just three people out of the forty-five I knew on the good side.

Now, I didn't just eliminate everybody in the bad column from my life. That's coldhearted, and I don't recommend anybody do that. I just slowly took inventory of who I needed to get closer to and who I needed to spend a little less time with. By spending more time with good influences, you'll naturally spend less time with the bad influences. That's how you need to handle it.

## OUR BEHAVIORS INFLUENCE OUR FAITH

We've discussed some of the obvious ways you can begin living by faith, like practicing gratitude, listing goals, and spending less time with negative influences. But other factors can influence your ability to live by faith in more subtle ways.

## THE NEWS FUELS YOUR NEGATIVE EMOTIONS

You need to be careful about the things you watch. Although it might sound extreme, I would recommend you stop looking at the news. I say this because I believe the news intentionally ties into your raw emotions and negative thinking so you'll talk about it and with other people. That discussion gives news channels more ratings.

Do you remember a news broadcast you watched in the past two weeks that didn't include something bad? There's a reason the saying "If it bleeds, it leads" is still heard in journalism schools. Most Americans just don't realize that the things they listen to and the people they're around influence their inner world, affecting what they achieve in their outer world.

## FEED YOUR BRAIN WHAT IT NEEDS

Music is another factor that influences your faith. "But Danny," you say, "I love music! You expect me to give it up?" Not quite, but you might want to shift your listening habits.

Right now, I'm committed to having a real estate portfolio of 1,000 doors, or 1,000 people or families who rent from me. Because I mostly deal with residential real estate, I don't know much about large, commercial buildings, so I've got to educate myself.

With that goal in mind, I've got two things I can do with my time when I have my headphones on at the gym or when I'm driving to work. I can listen to music, which I love. But the more I listen to songs, the more I memorize the words.

If I want to do something amazing in my life, like owning 1,000 doors, I don't have that much brain space for music. I'd rather spend my time listening to things related to buying commercial real estate. I'll find inspirational stories, or open my Audible app and buy a great audiobook. I'll listen to podcasts of people who've done what I want to do. I want to feed my mind the knowledge I'll need to be successful.

## FIND SUPPORT WITH A MASTERMIND GROUP

It's also essential that you create a mastermind group. To start that process, you should pick up any of the books from Napoleon Hill. He talks about the power of the mastermind group, and his books were instrumental in my life. The power of the mastermind group is simple. When you are trying to accomplish something and you have two or more like-minded individuals, people who think like you, you become twice as powerful.

If you have a goal to launch a business and be able to quit your job within two years, you're going to see clues along the way of things you could perceive are holding you back.

You're embarking into uncharted territory. You will exponentially increase your chances for success during that journey by surrounding yourself with three to five people who want to achieve something similar. When you have a question, doubt, fear, or worry, you can ask your mastermind group how they're dealing with it. Because they're in the same boat, they can tell you it's not a big deal, or show you how to move past the issue. Same thing on my end when they need help. That's the power of the mastermind group. It provides encouragement, guidance, and strength.

## HOW FAITH BREEDS RESILIENCY

All these activities will help you live by faith, which in turn will make you a more resilient person. Fear cripples you and doesn't allow you to move forward. When you're dealing in faith, you're empowered to move forward, and, with each step, you move closer to success. Faith gives you the ability to be resilient.

Not everybody owns a business because some people lack the resiliency to get through tough times. Why don't they have resiliency? They're crippled by fear, unable to move forward.

Many of you reading this book live in the United States, which I consider the greatest country on earth. There are people risking their lives traveling through shark-infested waters on boats made out of tires just to get to this country.

What makes them so resilient? Why don't they just turn back and go home? They persevere because they believe the United States holds the promise of a better life for their family. When you're living in faith and can see a greater future, nothing holds you back. You'll risk your life during a perilous journey to another country if that's what it takes. That is resiliency.

Let's say you've made all these changes and you're still stuck in fear right now. You're focusing on the positive, you've changed your listening habits, and you've created your own mastermind group, and yet you still can't embrace faith-based thinking fully. That's OK. You're not alone in that struggle. I want to share a very simple exercise I believe will help you get there.

I know what it's like when you're first starting in business. You worry if people are going to like you, if they're going to accept you, if you're good enough to do the job, all that stuff. I've had all those thoughts. It's a natural inclination we have as human beings to worry like that. What I want you to do right now is take a deep breath. We're going to work through some questions that will affirm your goodness.

*Are you a decent human being?*

If you're reading this book, I believe you're a decent human being.

*Do you mean well by people?*

Think about the promise of your business and the value you deliver to customers. Chances are good that you want to use that business to make the world a better place.

*Do you want to help other people?*

If you're in the service industry, do you genuinely want to help people save money on their taxes, have beautiful landscaping, be a better golfer? If you sell a product, is your desire to help customers make the best purchasing decision for their needs? If you search yourself and your goals, you'll realize you want, in every walk of life, to help people.

*Can people trust you?*

Good business practices, just like relationships, are built on trust. Are there people in your life who trust you? Friends, family members, a spouse, an employer, or a business partner? If you try your best to be trustworthy, it stands to reason that people will say they trust you.

*Can you be counted on?*

Does your boss count on you to show up for work on time? Does your spouse count on you to pick up the kids from school? Do your friends count on you for poker night or book club? When you go down the list, it's easy to see you're a person people can count on.

*Are you willing to work hard until the job gets done?*

If you're starting your own business, or already own one, there's no doubt you're willing to put in the required work. Just by reading this book, you're putting in extra work to improve yourself. The kind of person who quits before the job is done would never crack this book open.

Answering these questions is a powerful way to combat fear-based thinking. When you focus on the fear, you tend to forget who you are. These questions shift your perspective and help you remember that you're a great person who's willing to help a lot of people. If you answered yes to these questions, get out of your own way and go help people!

Fear-based thinking is debilitating no matter what you're trying to do with your life. You can't passively escape it, either. You have to make a conscious choice to shed your doubts and worries to become a more positive, optimistic person. Building your faith muscle through daily practice transforms you into someone who sees a brighter future and endless ways to get there. Your faith isn't blind. It's reaffirmed every time you take a step toward what you want.

Faith-based thinking provides the foundation for the six other principles of resiliency. Once you've laid that foundation, the next step is deciding what you want.

*Principle Two*

# DECIDE WHAT YOU WANT

· · · · · · ·

Are you destined for greatness?

I knew from an early age that I was destined to do great things far beyond the rough California neighborhood where I was raised. I had huge aspirations that drove me to work three jobs, seven days a week, until I made my dreams a reality.

However, there were times when I felt fear tugging at me, trying to drag me back down to where I started. As we discussed in the previous chapter, fear can be hard to shake once it grabs hold of you. Too many people have a difficult time deciding what they want because they're afraid of risk. That fear keeps them from venturing out and imagining what's possible for their life.

So how do you combat this fear?

You have to get a clear picture of what you want for your life. This grander vision will help you focus your efforts and serve as the guideline for everything else. It's going to pull you through the tough times. Without deciding what you want, you have nothing.

When I was young and hungry, with hardly any money to my name, I wanted to break free from the shackles of poverty and buy my mother a house. When I woke up every morning, that house—and everything it represented—was the first thing that crossed my mind. If you're going to make anything of yourself, you must have that same laserlike focus on your goal.

Once you get that vision, you'll start to think and make decisions based on what it takes to get there. If you step out as an entrepreneur, you're going to go through bumps and bruises. You're going to get beat up, metaphorically speaking. The thing that will help you get back up and keep going is that crystal clarity when it comes to what you want for your life or your career.

## BAKING YOUR WAY TO SUCCESS

Let me give you an example. We live in a world where somebody who's a good baker can start a baking blog and earn a full-time income—and then some—from the comfort of their own home, with just a laptop. This hypothetical individual has a dream to take what they know and teach it to others. That's called an information business.

Information businesses, which are made possible thanks to the Internet, are growing because people are looking for that information. They're looking for ways to do things in a better, more efficient manner. You can teach anything that you're really good at and passionate about and turn it into a business today. You can be free from having to work a job ever again, from missing your child's sporting event, or from ever having to say no to something because you don't have the time. But that all starts with first deciding what it is you want.

So, this hypothetical baker starts his information business on the Internet and has a goal to be the number one online authority for baking education. By deciding what he wants, this baker makes his "pie in the sky" goal seem less far-fetched. His plan is to charge people $25 a month to be a part of his subscription group. Eventually, he wants to have 5,000 subscribers and take in $125,000 a month, or $1.5 million per year.

Making over a million dollars a year teaching people how to bake is a lofty goal, right? No doubt! At first glance, that number seems unattainable. But that's what our baking friend wants for his life. To get there, he'll break the vision into bite-size pieces.

He decides that the first bite is getting 400 people to pay him $25 a month. That's $10,000 a month, or $120,000 a year. This not only replaces the baker's income, but puts some extra cash in his pocket to help his business reach the next level. So, there's his plan: find 400 people to pay him $25 a month. Conquer this bite and he can move on to the next one.

There's only one problem. Right now, the baker is thinking, "How on earth am I going to pull this off?" This is where most people stop. They can't overcome the question of how it's actually going to happen. The fear and the doubt start to creep in and they give up.

But not our brave baker! He's decided what he wants and that clarity allows him to see a way forward. He's going to focus on that first chunk.

The first step that he takes is getting a website. Then he adds some content to the website. Step number three is getting twenty people to pay him, let's say, $25 a month for access to his content. Once he gets twenty people, he sets his sights on fifty, then 100, and so on, until he hits 400. How fast he gets to 400 is solely dependent on how crystal clear his vision is and how much hard work he's willing to put into the vision.

On his journey to 400 subscribers, our baker will be actively marketing his site. He'll place some Facebook ads specifically targeted to people who want to learn how to bake. He'll host a webinar where he delivers baking instructions and promote that webinar on different blogs. Our baker will meet different podcast hosts and go on their shows, so that the audiences for those podcasts learn about him and what he does.

One tool he'll definitely have in his arsenal is a capture page that allows him to gather the names and e-mails of website visitors. This information allows him to build a list of people to market his blog to. What you need to understand is that everything this baker is doing can be done for a business idea you have. The key is to have a vision for what you want to accomplish. If you don't, you'll never start with that first step.

I want to challenge you here. In my example, why did I have to take the number down from 5,000 to 400? If you could get 400, couldn't you get 5,000? The answer is yes.

Why don't most people? Because they don't believe in the possibility. Four hundred is a number. Five thousand is a number. That's it. The only thing stopping you from running a $1.5 million a year business from your home with a laptop is the fear that keeps you from envisioning your ideal life. You conquer that fear by being crystal clear on what you want. That's when the planning can begin.

## FIND YOUR PASSION

Not only does a proper decision help you move forward, it also makes you a more resilient person. If you know what you want, then you know what you're working toward. It takes a lot of sacrifice to create a business and financial freedom. It really does. The only way to accomplish your goal is to figure out why you're doing it. That's when resilience is born.

If you're still unsure of how this process plays out, I'll give you another example, this time from my own professional journey. I had four reasons for opening my own real estate brokerage: I loved real estate, I loved people, I loved to see people succeed, and I believe I'm very good—the best in the country, in fact—at helping people succeed in the business of selling real estate. I had a passion that matched up perfectly with my skills. That was my vision.

When I put all those things together, opening my own brokerage felt like a no-brainer. I saw a definite void in the value that today's brokerages offered real estate professionals. I felt like the real estate community deserved more energy, passion, culture, coaching, and guidance when they're out building their businesses.

Here's a question for you: what void is there in your marketplace that you can fill? Do you have the confidence that I had when I was deciding to fill the void I saw in the real estate industry?

I knew I could do it. It became very evident to me that I was going to succeed at this endeavor because I knew what I wanted, I had confidence in my abilities, and I possessed a deep passion for helping other people. This is the magic formula for deciding what you want.

Let's walk through this formula step by step. The first step is to find out what you're good at and what you're passionate about. If something doesn't jump to mind, use this old test: if you never had to worry about money again, what would you do for a living?

Passions are wide-ranging; you could love helping people like I do, writing books, traveling, cooking, coaching sports, photographing nature, selling electronics, or playing video games competitively. It doesn't matter what you love to do, just that your passion for that activity is genuine and not a fleeting thrill. Take your time with this exercise if you need to, it because everything will unravel if you proceed any further without true passion.

The second thing you have to do is understand that everything around you—the pages of this book, the pen you're using to circle key words, the computer you might be typing on, the TV you may be looking at, even the walls around the room—started with an idea. Those ideas became a reality, and your ideas can become a reality as well.

Your idea doesn't have to be a technological innovation like the iPhone or a cure for cancer. It just needs to be an idea you believe in and desperately want to see come to fruition.

Once you find your passion and understand that everything starts with an idea, the third step is finding out how you can monetize what you're passionate about. As we discussed earlier in the example of the baker, anything that you can imagine can be monetized thanks to the Internet.

Chances are your idea won't make you rich right away. Finding new customers who are willing to take a chance on you, getting referrals, building a client base through word of mouth—these things take time. You can't be serious about changing your life if you think you're going to get rich overnight. If that's your desire, go play the lottery. We're talking about using our passion to create a business and earn financial freedom. Patience and persistence are crucial.

When you take what you're passionate about and add that to a compensation model, the last question you have to ask yourself is, "What do I need to earn to make myself financially free and do this on a full-time basis?" You give yourself a time frame: "I'm going to accomplish this within $x$ amount of time." The goals need to be specific and have a time stamp on them.

Don't worry if you still have questions. The next chapter is all about making a plan.

## HOP INTO YOUR TIME MACHINE

I want to share a tool with you that I've used before to envision my ideal life. It might sound crazy at first, but just hear me out. To achieve clarity, you need to step into your time machine and jump ten years into the future. (I told you it was a little wacky!) This is an exercise I like to call "Future You."

Looking at yourself in the future, what have you accomplished? How would you describe your lifestyle? What type of home do you live in? How do you spend your time? What's your income? How has your family benefited from the choices you've made?

These are questions to ask yourself in your time machine. If you can envision yourself ten years down the road, living your ideal life, the answer to what you really want will hit you right between the eyes. To guide your time jump, I want you to examine your ideal life in seven areas: family, mind-set/beliefs, business, contribution, fitness, income, and wealth creation/personal finance.

### FAMILY

If you're a provider for your family, step number one is deciding what kind of lifestyle you want to provide them. I list this component first because family is the most important part of my life, and I want to share an example of how my time machine influenced my family.

Just today, we poured the concrete for our new home. I always wanted a large piece of land where my kids could run around and have fun. When did I decide that? Ten years ago. I actually drew a picture of the type of home and space I wanted to have for my family.

Sure enough, three years ago, we bought a piece of land. It was a little over an acre. Today, the workers poured the foundation, and next week the frame will go up. Ten years ago, I used my time machine to crystallize in my mind the house I wanted my family to have. Time traveling into the future is not some silly, hypothetical exercise. I wouldn't waste your time like that.

What we're doing is no different than what quarterbacks do before the big game, when they envision the game plan unfolding in real time on the field. They visualize the wide receivers running their routes, and they go through their reads on each play. If the defense presents a certain look, the quarterback practices calling another play. He is quite literally seeing his future. If you asked any professional quarterback about this practice, he'd say it was key to his success.

What we're doing is envisioning our own success, and it starts with providing for our family.

## MIND-SET/BELIEFS

What you believe is possible dictates all aspects of your life. So your number one priority, besides your family, should be to grow in the area of mental strength. The more you expand your mind and deepen your self-belief, the more you can accomplish.

Do you know how many more Mark Zuckerbergs are out there in the world? I believe there are millions of them. The difference was that Mark Zuckerberg refused to believe that Facebook would not become a reality. In his mind, it already existed, and his job was to reverse engineer the pieces that would comprise his world-changing idea.

Same with Steve Jobs, who was a maniacal perfectionist. If you haven't read about his routine before revealing a new Apple product, you really should. Steve Jobs knew how his company's products could change people's lives, and he wanted nothing more than to help them see what he saw. His focus and vision are what made him such a brilliant innovator. Talk about somebody who knew exactly what he wanted, why he wanted it, and most importantly, somebody who didn't wonder if the public wanted it as well.

In fact, Jobs is famous for saying, "The public doesn't even know what they want until we give it to them." He had a crystal clear vision for what he wanted—to work with the best people, to use the best materials for his products, and to actualize ideas that very few people could even fathom. His commitment to his vision enabled him to change the world. When you look into the future, make sure you've developed the kind of leadership skills that Steve Jobs possessed and have increased your capacity to believe in possibilities for your life. You won't make a lot of money or advance in life if you're not continually improving your mind-set and sharpening your beliefs.

## BUSINESS

Let's look at the creation of my brokerage to examine why it's important to envision your business in the future. Like most new companies, no one had ever heard of us when we first opened. People couldn't even pronounce the name.

From day one, I wanted Intero to first be the number one office in our city, then in our region, then in the state, and then in the country. I wanted to be number one because winning is important to me. I realize winning isn't everything to everybody, and if that's you, I want to challenge you to find what is important to you. If winning isn't your motivator, then what will fuel you to push past some of the natural setbacks that happen in business? What's going to motivate and inspire you to give it your best on a day-to-day basis?

Winning for me started with being the best brokerage in our city, which meant I had to answer one simple question: who was number one currently? I learned everything about the top brokerage and then put pen to paper and wrote out what we had to do to become number one and take that prize from the current top dog.

Once we achieved that, I set our sights on conquering the region, which is one of the biggest counties in California. Despite the increased geographical size and the new pool of competitors, our process didn't change. I applied the same tactics that made us number one in our city, as we fought to conquer the region and become the top producing brokerage in Southern California.

Notice that I didn't want to be number one in the state right away, choosing instead to focus on conquering our city at first. I did this because I'd rather set a goal I can hit, while still being challenged, than set a crazy goal I'll never reach.

When you set a goal, create a plan, and then actually achieve it, that victory reinforces the notion that you're a winner who follows through on commitments. Once you start hitting your targets consistently, an inner belief begins to build that says you can achieve whatever goal you set for yourself. If you want to be successful, that inner belief is indispensable. Without it, you'll find it difficult to win in business.

With our collective belief, we quickly became the top office in Rancho Cucamonga, and now we're number three in Southern California after four years.

Being able to achieve your goals and build that inner belief comes down to hunger. You've got to be hungry to accomplish something, to prove someone wrong, be the best in your industry...whatever it is, you've got to be hungry about something.

Sitting in my office during those early days, I foresaw a future where our agency sold more homes than any agency in the country. I shared my vision with everyone who came to work with me, and, together, we pushed ahead toward that inevitable future.

Do you like how I used the word *inevitable* when describing my company's future? I have confidence in my time machine! The future doesn't lie.

## CONTRIBUTION

There's a saying I like to borrow from my pastor: "Biblical abundance means that abundance flows through you and then to others, not to you." You'll receive a new kind of power once you understand this truth.

Here's another saying: "At the end of the day people won't remember what you said or did; they will remember how you made them feel." That one is from Maya Angelou.

When I talk about your contribution, I don't mean what you add to your company's bottom line or how much money you put into your family's bank account. I want you to envision how you can help other people accomplish what they want. This is the true definition of success.

Unfortunately, we live in a world where everybody's just thinking about themselves and the measure of success has become distorted. It's not about owning a yacht or a vacation home; it's about making the lives of everyone around you better. When you achieve success, you have an obligation to allow the good things in your life to flow to those around you. That's the truth at the core of those previous quotes: be a river, not a dam.

You should strive to build a company whose spirit, energy, and passion bless the lives of others and whose products and services impact people in a positive way. When you do that, your business becomes an unstoppable force for good. With Intero, I won't hire salespeople with selfish attitudes, no matter how much they produce. I want team members who will share secrets of success with newcomers.

My hiring stance was tested, but I stood firm, because I wanted a company culture focused on contribution. If my people contributed more to others than to themselves, I knew the lives of everyone in our company would be blessed.

Think about yourself in that way. How can you create something so special that people can't help but smile when they walk through your doors?

Seek to become an unstoppable force for good in your personal and professional life.

## FITNESS

You perform better when you feel better. You'll struggle to become a peak-performing individual until you grapple with this fact. If you don't take care of yourself physically, you're going to feel terrible and your ability to succeed in other areas will suffer.

You have to decide that you want to be a "great being." What is a great being? It starts with first taking care of your mind and your soul, which we already covered, then taking care of your body.

I'm a big believer in this philosophy. I wake up every morning between 3:30 and 3:45, and I'm at the gym by 4:30. I'm in my office by 7:45, while most people are dragging to get to work at 9:00. Seeing the positive impact this routine has made on my life, I know it could help other people.

That's why I encourage all the agents in my company to join me at the gym. Sure enough, every day we have fifty to sixty people wake up and join me for an early morning workout.

This one change has made a profound difference. On the low end, I've seen a 40 percent increase in productivity and income. On the high end, in one case, we had an 8,000 percent increase from one year to the next, just because of that one change. I'm not kidding!

You've got to light that fire. Most Americans are living in a coma, floating through life with no idea of what's going on. That doesn't have to be you. If you commit to making that change, I guarantee you will see the results spilling into other aspects of your life.

To get started, decide what time you're going to wake up every day. It doesn't have to be as early as I wake up. You could get up thirty minutes earlier than you do now if that's easier. Whatever you decide, commit to doing it five days a week.

The second step is doing something active every day. It could be walking your dog or going for a run. If you need accountability, join a gym with some friends.

Don't be too attached to what you do or how early you do it. Getting started is the key. Commit to doing something five days a week and build the habit from there.

I love starting off my day knowing I'm doing something that must people would never consider doing. It's a powerful psychological motivator.

## INCOME

The first thing I want to establish here is that money is energy. Let me repeat that: *money is energy*. Money is simply the reward you receive for the value that you give to the world. This means if you currently don't have money, you're not bringing enough value to the world. That's why we're talking about it after we discuss your contribution. Once you take care of all the other areas, money becomes a natural by-product.

Most people mess up when they put money first in their priorities. They worry about how much money they're going to make. Those people end up getting divorced because they didn't put their family first. Those people get sick and stressed out because they didn't put their health first. You're going to suffer if your priorities aren't in line.

Once your priorities are straight, you can achieve whatever income goals you set for yourself if you can master the art of tracking your progress.

I learned to value tracking in high school when I was wrestling and made a goal to win thirty-five matches. I put the number 35 at the top of a piece of paper and circled it. Then I recorded the results for every match and tournament on that page. I was excited to come home from a wrestling tournament, because I couldn't wait to add another point to my sheet and see how much closer I was getting to thirty-five. As those points increased, so did my excitement for the next match.

As an eighteen-year-old kid living in a two-bedroom apartment with a mother on welfare, tracking my progress was a difference that made a difference. I'm still tracking my progress to this day, because I know I can earn whatever I want to earn. I simply have to be clear about what I want and hold myself accountable to that.

## WEALTH CREATION/PERSONAL FINANCE

You might be wondering, how is this different from income? To put it simply, income is what you earn, and wealth is what you do with what you earn.

You could be an NFL player and go bankrupt, which 80 percent of all NFL players do three years after retirement. If you don't have a plan for wealth creation, then the same thing could happen to you.

My simple plan for wealth creation is as follows:

- How much does it take me to live?
- How much can I realistically earn this year?

If I subtract how much I'm going to earn from how much it costs me to live, I'm going to have excess. Then I put a plan together to invest that excess, and my vehicle of choice is obviously real estate. After that, I calculate how many apartment buildings I have to buy to free my family financially.

What does it mean to be financially free?

It means having the same or more passive revenue coming in every month than your monthly bills, with or without you working. In other words, you have enough passive residual income to cover your monthly overhead. Once you do that, then you are legitimately free in a financial sense. That's how to make your income work for you.

As a real estate guy, I'd recommend investing in real estate. If this process intimidates you, start small. That's what

I did when I purchased my first investment property—a little condo worth $100,000 that I got for $50,000. Now my goal is to own 100 doors, but I started with a condo that I paid off and still own. It pays us $1,000 a month in rent.

If you're interested in growing your wealth, whether through real estate or another vehicle, what's holding you back from making your first investment? If it's fear, here are a few steps for overcoming that negative emotion and starting to grow your wealth:

1. Calculate how much residual income you can realistically create for yourself in the next twenty-four months.
2. Decide what investment vehicle is best suited for you.
3. Identify how much money you need to save to buy the assets that will allow you to start creating residual income.
4. Develop action steps that will create the confidence you need to do what you want to do. Do you need to take a class or hire a coach before getting started?
5. Put some accountability in place for yourself. Tell your goal to someone who can light a fire under you and push you to get the job done.

## A NEGATIVE NET WORTH

Now that you've jumped into your time machine and examined Future You, I want to conclude this chapter with another story from my professional journey. Because we were just talking about wealth, this story is particularly appropriate.

I was three years into the real estate business and making between $125,000 and $150,000 a year at ages eighteen, nineteen, and twenty. I thought I was Mr. Hotshot. Life was great. After all, nobody's out there making that kind of money at my age, right? At least nobody in my neighborhood.

I'll never forget what happened next. I went to a seminar and heard two words mentioned that I had never heard before in my life: *net worth.* The guy at this seminar asked the audience, "What is your net worth?" Here I am, Mr. Hotshot. I'm a young guy making six figures. Nobody could stop me. I can't wait to answer because I know my net worth is really high.

The speaker told us we could figure out our net worth by taking the assets we own—real estate, stock, savings, an investment portfolio—and subtracting from that the liabilities that we owe. I did the math and I thought something was wrong. My net worth was negative $32,000!

This meant that, to die in peace, I would have to come up with $32,000 to pay somebody back. I thought to myself,

"Whoa! Wait a minute. This is impossible. This is not me. I'm a winner." But I realized that I was currently losing in this area of my life, and one thing that I hate more than anything is losing.

So what did I do? I set a goal. But not just any goal: I set an audacious goal. I followed the exact steps that I'm teaching you to follow right now.

Step number one was deciding exactly what I wanted. At that seminar, I knew there were about twenty people who had a net worth of at least $1 million, because they raised their hand when the speaker asked how many people had that kind of net worth.

I thought to myself that if they could do it, I could do it, too.

The second step was putting together a plan of action. It broke my goal down into bite sizes. I gave myself twenty-four months to be worth $1 million.

To get started, I thought about what I had to be worth in six months, twelve months, and eighteen months to be within striking distance of $1 million net worth in twenty-four months. I put those targets down on an Excel spreadsheet and then got to work.

The first thing I did was start paying off all the debt that I owed as fast as humanly possible. I was obviously making a good income. It's just that I was doing dumb things with that income. So I eliminated my debt and cleaned up my spending habits.

Twenty-five months later, I was worth $1 million.

I don't want to make it seem like your goals have to be related to money. Years after I made that net worth goal, I was single and wanted to find a great wife. To find a great wife, I knew I needed to first become a great suitor, a great man.

I started to write down the things that I felt would make me attractive to the kind of woman that I was looking for, one with confidence and values, a woman I could trust, a woman who could trust me, and so on.

Raising my net worth to $1 million wasn't about the money for me. It was about the commitment to a goal. The same truth applied here. I had to make myself the kind of man who would attract a great spouse. I didn't want a crappy relationship. I didn't want to deal with instability or divorce, or go through not being able to trust my spouse.

To avoid all of that, I first had to become a different type of person. I had to become trustworthy, show that I was responsible, and exude confidence.

We can take that idea and apply it to this entire process. The end goal is that you're going to live financially free, but it's not really about the money. It's about your commitment to the process of being a better human being, of working on your mind-set, of not being afraid of what you want or being afraid of taking risks. If you commit to improving in these ways, the money will be the reward for your journey.

After you've started living by faith instead of fear, it's time to decide what you want. A plane doesn't fly without a destination, just like a quarterback doesn't make a pass without an intended receiver. Before you can begin making a plan, you have to know where you want to end up. You know your starting point—where you are now—and now you just need an endpoint. Once you have it, you can begin to chart your journey between the two.

That's when the fun begins.

*Principle Three*

# MAKE A PLAN

. . . . . . .

My friend Travis was a man without a plan.

When we first met, I noticed how willing he was to accept mediocrity in his life. He worked nights at Target and came to me for coaching during the day. I thought we were making progress on those days when Travis left my office inspired and motivated to change his life.

But I soon realized what I was telling him went in one ear and out the other. The rut he'd dug for himself was nice and comfortable. He had no idea what he wanted out of life and had no plan to create a better future for himself. Simply put, Travis was a man adrift.

In succumbing to the stories he told himself, Travis couldn't imagine living a better life outside his current situation. He desperately needed someone to confront the thinking that had guided him to this point. That moment came one day during a coaching session, when Travis said, "I've come to my wit's end, Danny. Today I had to steal money from my son's piggy bank just to fill up my gas tank. I am done. Tell me what to do. Please help me." I told him I wouldn't help him, and he asked why not.

"Because you love being broke and miserable!" I replied.

Travis was indignant. He acted like he had no idea what I was talking about. I knew this moment could be a turning point in his life if I convinced him to get out of his rut, decide what he wanted, and make a plan for how to get there. I told him I would prove that he loved being broke.

"Travis, when your hair gets long and bushy, and it starts itching the back of your neck, what do you do?" I asked him. He told me he got a haircut. Next, I asked him what he would do if he ate too much and his clothes didn't fit anymore. "I'd eat better and I'd go work out," he answered.

Now we were getting somewhere.

"When you really want something to change, you go out and fix it. You don't accept mediocrity. The reason you had to steal from your son's piggy bank is that you are perfectly fine with your mediocre life. If you wanted a better life, you would've done something to fix it by now."

I asked Travis to repeat a phrase, which he didn't want to do at first. I'm so glad I pushed him because it was a life-changing moment for Travis and for me, because I learned what tough leadership was all about.

Finally, he said it: "I love being broke."

He said it three times before we both got emotional. In that moment, we realized he wasn't meant for such a miserable life. He was meant for greatness.

Travis just needed to vocalize what was lurking in his subconscious the entire time. Once he heard himself say the words, he decided that wasn't who he wanted to be, neither for his family nor for his future. It was the beginning of his breakthrough.

Before that moment, Travis had never looked at his life in that way. He was simply living day by day, doing what had to be done to provide for his family. He never considered that his life could be more than a stagnant real estate career and nights spent at Target. This realization was a gut punch, and we both got emotional right there in my office. But I needed to be tough with him, so he could see what his life had become. In that moment, he gained the clarity needed to change his life.

## CHARTING YOUR COURSE

Deciding that you're fed up with where you are in life and resolving to make a change can be a sobering moment, but I promise you, that's when the fun really begins.

You can sit down and start to plan, step by step, how to get what you want. Envisioning the path to your ideal life can unleash the spirit that's been locked up by your damaging beliefs. Unlocking the spirit brings about new hope, clarity, and belief. When you can align those three things through a plan, things start to change in your life.

Your plan starts with understanding your destination. You might target a particular profit margin, crave a certain lifestyle, or strive to create a legacy that can be passed down to your children. Whatever your goal, it needs to be crystal clear in your mind.

Your goal becomes crystal clear when you say it aloud or write it down multiple times a day. Daily journaling is a great way to reinforce faith in your vision. Although belief comes slowly at first, building your faith muscle through daily reps strengthens your ability to believe.

But you must be willing to do the work if you want to see results.

That's step number one in making a plan, and it's a crucial step.

Step two is to go back to your goal and make it bigger. Your decision-making process is based on your current scope of reality, so whatever you think is big right now, you need to stretch it. If you execute your plan correctly, you'll outgrow any goal you set that was based on your narrow perception of what is possible for your life at this moment.

I've seen this in my own life during phone conversations with my coach, whom I've been working with for four years. During one of our first coaching calls, I set a goal for our company to sell 500 homes in a year. When she read that back to me recently, I started laughing. This year, our company is going to sell 4,000 homes! I didn't know it at the time, but my dreams were way too small.

They were small because of my life perspective in that moment, not because I was afraid to achieve greatness. I wasn't as confident in my abilities as a business person yet, so my faith muscle wasn't as developed and my goals were small.

You have no idea what your capabilities could be five or six years from now, so instead of wasting time finding out, stretch yourself today by doubling your goal.

After starting small, my new goal is for our company to sell 20,000 homes in a year. That sounds insane, right? Think about it this way: after five years, we are selling nearly eight times as many homes as I hoped we would when I made that original goal.

We've experienced this insane growth because I worked toward my plan every day, through one battle after another. Sometimes those battles were mental, and other times they were brought on by challenging people or bad market conditions. As you grow your business, you'll also grow as a human being. It's a beautiful thing, but it doesn't happen overnight. You must be patient with the process.

My growth has allowed me to expand the scope of what I think is possible, and I have no doubt our company can make that kind of jump. I encourage you to do the same when you're making your plan and setting goals for where you want to be in one, five, or ten years. Don't limit yourself: dream big!

## MAKE TIME FOR NEW BUSINESS

Once you've decided what you want and have stretched it, you must learn to guide your actions to make your plan work. Time management is especially important for people who are starting their businesses part-time, those with another job or a family to support. If you're in that situation, you can't use other aspects of your life as an excuse not to execute your plan. Rather, you must use your family or the desire to work full-time in your dream job as motivation to maximize the hours you dedicate to your business.

Time management is crucial when you're starting out, because you'll wear every hat for your business: CEO, janitor, accountant, marketer, and so on. You have very little leverage in the early stages, aside from your output and the ability to give maximum effort.

With a small business, you also have to set aside time for lead generation. Your process will differ from that of large companies like Coca-Cola or Apple, which use their massive marketing budgets to communicate directly with their target audience and generate new business. When you have a small or nonexistent marketing budget, how can you drum up new business?

You find new business in one of two ways:

- It comes to you.
- You go get it.

That's it. To go one step further, there are two types of people to get business from:

- People you know
- People you don't know

It doesn't get much simpler than that, does it?

I know some people get anxious at the thought of talking to new people. To be really honest with you: you have to get over it. You've got a lot of money, time, and energy invested in what you're trying to accomplish, so the stakes are very high.

To get business from people you don't know, you have to get "belly to belly" or "ear to ear." *Belly to belly* means getting in front of people to talk about your products or services. *Ear to ear* is the same thing, but over the phone.

You have to go out and meet people and talk to them, which is an area where I think most people struggle. Savvy entrepreneurs understand that prospecting strangers is part of the sacrifice demanded by success. It's common sense when you think about it: there are more people you don't know than people you do know. That means eventually you're going to have to communicate in some way with people you don't know.

The sooner you make that leap, the better.

## INVESTING MORE THAN JUST MONEY

People think it's enough to sacrifice by putting money into their business, signing a lease, buying furniture, or creating a logo. That's all the foundational stuff that gets you in the door. The real question is what are you going to do to drive people to take a look at that snazzy logo, sit on the immaculate furniture, and check out your new location?

The answer is lead generation.

The first method of lead generation is to wait for the business to come to you. You can grab a great location, put out a big, flashing sign, and hope someone visits you. Although this strategy can work, it's usually when you've invested millions in a prime location where customers go to find businesses like yours. Think about car dealerships.

I've never used this approach and don't recommend it.

The second method is to buy business through advertising and marketing. One game-changer in this realm is Facebook advertising, which allows you to target specific groups of people on Facebook. Rather than sinking money into billboards or TV commercials, you should connect with a Facebook advertising specialist and begin running ads.

Instagram has also changed the game for small businesses, particularly in the clothing industry. Large brands like Ralph Lauren and Gap are still around, but they're losing market share to small brands that start out in garages posting pictures of clothes on Instagram and selling direct to consumer. Like Facebook, you can run targeted ads on Instagram or hire someone to help you target customers on this platform.

The third method is near and dear to my heart—generating business yourself. This method allowed me to create three businesses that generated $1,000,000 or more in revenue, yet few want to use this method because they think it's difficult.

Generating leads through prospecting will add the most profit to your business, but it also involves confrontation and rejection, which scares people to death. They'd rather pay for ads than talk to people on the phone or meet them face-to-face.

In real estate, we use two different types of prospecting:

- Phone calls to a targeted list of potential consumers
- Door knocking in high-turnover neighborhoods

When I used to knock on doors, I thought it was the best thing since apple pie. I'd get into the office around 8:00 a.m. and practice what I'd say for thirty minutes. Then I'd hit the streets and knock on doors from 9:00 a.m. to noon. I loved it, yet everyone thought I was nuts.

I always told them I was getting paid while I exercised and got a tan. How could you beat that? I didn't want to knock on doors for the rest of my life, but starting out in business with little leverage, it was the quickest way for me to spread the word.

Let me give you an example of how to generate leads for a new business. Say I decided to open a new ice-cream shop tomorrow. My first step would be to load up my car with coolers full of ice cream, pay a couple buddies to come with me, and hit every business in town giving out free samples. If they wanted more, we'd sell to them on the spot. In each business, I'd also give out a coupon that enticed people to visit our shop.

My goal would be to talk with 100 people every day, five days a week. If you kept that up for an entire year, you would talk with 24,000 potential customers. What do you think would happen in my first year of business if I talked to 24,000 people with a smile on my face and love in my heart? I think I'd be the number one ice-cream shop in town.

You can't be afraid of hard work and rejection. Some people will like what you offer and others won't, but that's not important. The vision you have for your business is what's important. When you remember that, lead generation becomes less scary.

For all the success I've enjoyed, I still have to generate new business. The podcast I recently started called *The Danny Morel Show* cracked the top 100 business podcasts on iTunes and averaged 2,000 downloads weekly after just thirty days.

I'd never had my own podcast before, so I was in uncharted territory when it came to lead generation. I didn't let that intimidate me, though. I attracted new listeners by talking about the podcast on social media and sharing it with everybody I knew. Once I saw our initial success, I started placing strategic ads to get people to give me a shot. I knew once they listened to the podcast, they'd love it, and our audience would grow.

If you attack new challenges with fearlessness, I'm confident you'll find similar success.

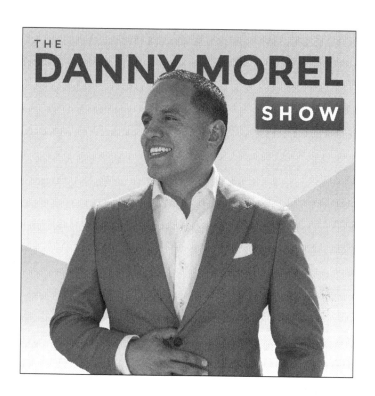

THE
**DANNY MOREL**
SHOW

## YOU HAVE TO FEEL GOOD TO PERFORM WELL

Some entrepreneurs need an hour-by-hour schedule to make sure they're checking all the boxes to grow their business. I don't think you need to restrict yourself that much and would instead recommend time blocking. There are key things you need to accomplish to succeed, and you should block out time for those key things each day.

During my typical workday, I'll block out time to work out in the morning, generate new leads, follow up with existing leads, take care of my to-do activities, work on my presentations, and negotiate offers. I don't need to schedule those items hour by hour. Rather, I know going into my day that I'm not finished until all these items have received my attention.

Do you want to know which of those activities I would never leave off my daily schedule? Based on what we just talked about, you'd probably say "lead generation."

You'd be wrong.

Although daily lead generation is crucial, I can't function if I don't start my day with some sort of physical activity. If you want to know a commonality among high achievers, it's a commitment to daily exercise. They believe, like I do, that feeling good about yourself is half the battle. You perform better when you feel good.

Whether it's walking, lifting weights, or taking a Zumba class, do something that gets you up and excited about the day. If you're not a "fitness person," you might think I'm just some fitness nut and wonder how this principle applies to you. For me, including fitness in my day is crucial, because it represents something more important than getting in shape.

To illustrate this point, I want you to picture Navy SEALs boot camp in your mind. Even if you've never been in the Navy SEALs or seen this training in action, you can imagine just how grueling it is. You're not picturing the Navy SEALs waking up at 10:00 a.m. and spending the day drinking beer and eating pizza. There aren't any stories of all-day Navy SEALs barbeques. A drill sergeant wakes Navy SEALs up at 3:30 a.m., and they endure the strictest discipline imaginable in terms of their diet, exercise, and daily routine. Discipline and precision are drilled into them, because there's no room for error when their lives are on the line. Boot camp trains Navy SEALs to bring out the best version of themselves.

Navy SEALs can't leave anything to chance when they're put to the test, so they willingly put in the work so to make sure they're 100 percent ready for game day.

Are you ready for game day in your business? Because this same idea applies to entrepreneurs. The reality is that businesses succeed or fail because of people who make important decisions. The people making those decisions need to work at becoming the best people they can be.

Who will most likely perform better? The person who sleeps in or the person who wakes up early? The person who does some sort of workout, or the person who skips it because it's not a priority for them? The person who eats a well-balanced diet filled with lean meats, fruits, and vegetables, or the person who drinks Coca-Cola and eats candy and pizza every day?

As the leader of a company, I want the people who work for me to see someone who is constantly striving for greatness in every area of his life. A focus on fitness also builds mental toughness. When the going gets tough, which it often does in business, you can fall back on those small victories you win each day. Even if that victory is as small as waking up consistently, you're proving something important to yourself.

## MOVING FORWARD DESPITE TOUGH CIRCUMSTANCES

Every aspect of your plan, including fitness, is going to make you a more resilient person, because a plan is more than just putting one step after another on the way to success. Your plan gives you a target and a focus. Most importantly, it gives you hope.

There will be months when you can't pay your employees or don't bring in the revenue you expected. The hope provided by your plan will keep you going amid those tough circumstances. If you constantly remind yourself of your plan by writing it down or visualizing it, I promise it will eventually lead you to success, despite the obstacles and naysayers trying to slow you down.

In other words, a plan makes you tenacious.

Tenacity is one of the qualities I believe makes the United States the greatest country in the world. Our country never gives up, and yet I see surrender everywhere I look. We live in the richest country in the world—the land of opportunity—but millions of people have succumbed to daily routine because nothing about their life excites them.

They work Monday to Friday, nine-to-five, barbeque on weekends, then get up the next week and do it all over again. Could there be anything more soul-crushing for the human spirit than a decade of that monotony?

We're living at a point in time where it's never been easier to start the company of your dreams. Anything you want for your life, your business, and your legacy is possible, but you've got to believe that. I definitely believe that's true, and if you're with me, let's take a look at the personnel you'll need to identify in your plan.

## SURROUND YOURSELF WITH THE RIGHT PEOPLE

A good plan starts with your leadership. When I started my company, I filled every role over the course of some very long eighteen-hour days. Despite the grueling hours and thankless tasks like cleaning floors, I did every job to the best of my ability. Setting a standard for excellence was important, because I knew someday I'd be able to bring on other people to fill those roles. The only way they would do their job to the level I expected would be if I personally knew it could be done at that level.

Therefore, I encourage you to begin your plan with a clear understanding of what your process will be like and how the roles in your company should be performed.

You then want to define the job you're looking to fill within the context of your company's structure. In other words, before you ever bring a person onto your team, you first have to map out what your organization will look like going forward.

So many business owners just hire people. I don't hire people; I fill positions that fit specifically in the blueprint for my organization. You have to keep in mind that people are people, and every person you know is going to let you down at some point. The flip side of that is that sometimes people are going to surprise or inspire you by what they're able to do. I think the key, specifically for small business owners, is not to simply hire people, but to fill positions with the right people for the job.

Creating an organizational chart of your company will help you see what positions you need to hire. Once you find the positions needed to fulfill your plan, create a detailed description for each one. These descriptions should include the qualifications that person's going to need, the tasks they'll be expected to accomplish, and the type of personality that would be ideal in that position. If you begin your search with specific details, it'll be like the right person just appears out of thin air.

I've seen it happen time and time again. It's amazing.

I shared some words with you before we started chapter 1 that I have framed in my office. I want to revisit those words now, to show you so more of what is written there, and to examine how they helped guide me as I planned my company. Again, these were words that I penned before I hired a soul to work for me:

*Who are we? We are a place of change, we are a place of breakthroughs, we are a place of growth. We take people who can't see, and we help them to see. Once they can see, then they start to believe. When they believe, they start to take inspired action. Once they take inspired action, they step into living the life they were destined to live. We are a life and business development company that focuses on helping our clients and agents live abundant lives in these five areas: family, mind and body, spiritual, contribution, and financial freedom.*

That's who we are as an organization. By committing to that vision from the start, I had a standard I could use to measure every aspect of my plan. I knew what roles needed to be filled, because I could see where my company's needs would be. Then, by working in those roles myself, I established a high standard across the board that I knew would set my company apart.

After writing out my vision, I was able to pen the following words, which define the ideal agent at our real estate brokerage:

*First and foremost, a humble heart and spirit. A team player who thrives being around others and their energy, who keeps their ego in check enough to coexist with other top-producing individuals. Someone who has a deep desire to win, and win big, and someone who understands that the best way to win is to surround yourself with winners. A person with high ethics and integrity, who doesn't focus on their commission, but realizes that the secret to success*

*in sales is to help as many people as possible achieve what
they want, and as a result, compensation will never be
an issue.*

I'll ask you now: Who are you? What does your business
stand for and what does it do? What value does your business bring to the community?

Your plan must include a clear answer to these questions.

## GET TO KNOW YOUR CUSTOMERS

Once you understand your company at its very core, then
it's time to get acquainted with your ideal customer. Ask
yourself the following questions to guide this process:

- What does your ideal customer want?
- How can your business fulfill those needs?
- What kind of income does your ideal customer earn?
- How much of that income can they spend on services like
  yours?
- How do they treat you? How do you treat them?
- What maintains your relationship with these ideal
  customers?

The more detailed you get, the better off you'll be. Bad
companies don't attract bad customers, but rather the

wrong customers. They either haven't identified their ideal customer or, if they have, they're not communicating their message very effectively. Companies that end up in this position close long before their potential is fulfilled.

You know a good way to figure out what your ideal customer looks like? Getting belly to belly! By meeting new people and talking to them about your business, you see the ones who naturally gravitate toward your product or service. Did the golfer from the country club seem disinterested, but the truck driver you met at the gas station was eating out of the palm of your hand? These little interactions provide important clues you should take into consideration.

Customers are the lifeblood of your company, the conduits through which all your desired results will flow. I would therefore urge you to take your time and give significant thought to these questions, because they'll help you conceptualize your customer profiles.

After all, no plan can survive if your business shuts down due to a lack of customers.

## REPEL THE WRONG PEOPLE

Knowing what your organization is all about and envisioning your ideal customer is important, because this helps you attract the right people and situations to fulfill your vision. Conversely, it helps you repel people and situations that are wrong for your business. Let me give you a couple of examples to explain what I mean.

We recently held our second annual yearly event for small business owners, called "Relentless," which I hope to see you at one day. (For more information, visit www.Danny-Morel.com) We hired a guest speaker we thought would be a fantastic addition to our event. But once we signed the agreement and started planning, something happened.

We noticed that our business principles were out of alignment with the speaker's principles, which made him a bad fit for our event. That didn't mean he was a bad person or a terrible speaker, but merely the wrong choice to convey the message we were so passionate about. We parted ways and found another speaker.

Had we not been crystal clear about what our organization and our event stood for, we might not have spotted this problem, and the participants whose lives we hoped to change would not have gotten the "relentless experience" we intended.

Take a moment and honestly examine your business. Do you have the right people involved, or are there employees who don't fit your culture? If so, what's stopping you from releasing those people? It's a tough decision, but at Intero, I let go of salespeople who don't want to bring energy, passion, and joy to the workplace. I decided long ago that those three traits would define our culture, and I don't let anyone sabotage that.

If you haven't started a business yet, you've got a leg up. You can save yourself a lot of heartbreak by defining your business culture and envisioning your ideal customer.

### HOW TRAVIS CHANGED HIS LIFE

When we left my friend Travis, he was on the verge of realizing his true potential. But first he needed a plan to provide him with a target, focus, and hope. Here's the plan he came up with that completely changed his life for the better.

First, he decided he wanted to leave Target and work in his real estate business full time. He felt that doing so would allow him to close twenty transactions a year, which would have brought him between $160,000 and $180,000 in income. So, of course, I helped him stretch his goal to thirty deals and $250,000 in income. You have to dream big!

Next, Travis considered how he would find new business. Because he was serious about reaching his goal, Travis committed to go knock on doors two hours a day, five days a week. But because Travis is human, he needed a few nudges to stay on track.

When we started tracking his numbers, I knew from my own experience that he could easily make ten contacts an hour knocking on doors. Yet Travis was only speaking to two people an hour. I knew something was wrong. Either the conversations he was having were too long, or he wasn't focused. Sure enough, he was taking phone calls during his door-knocking window.

Once we refocused him, he took off like a rocket.

Travis started working on his presentation, developing his skill set, and honing his process to become a more efficient real estate agent. That first year, he closed something like twenty-four deals. Within three months, he was able to quit Target completely and go full time with real estate.

I have so many stories of people like Travis who utterly transformed their lives, but I wanted to share his particular journey with you because I think it speaks to our ability to come back from rock bottom. Travis hit that low point when he sobbed in my office about stealing from his son's piggy bank. He was sick and tired of the life he was living and knew there was more out there for him.

## EMBRACE YOUR PLAN

Are you in a place similar to Travis that day he wept in my office? If so, I think it's time you shed your broken-down life and moved full steam ahead toward your ideal future. It's time for you to live by faith, decide what you want, and make a plan to get there.

A plan is like a roadmap: it shows you how to get to your ideal future from where you are now. You'll still hit some bumps and run over some potholes along the way, but now you'll know what's waiting on the other side of those obstacles.

A plan is also like a blueprint in that it lays out the entire vision for your company or your new life. It's much easier to make informed decisions when you have the full picture. Hiring people or making important life choices without the benefit of context is a risk you don't have to take.

Most importantly, a plan is your safety net for when times get tough. I've had those days when low revenue made me question everything. I've stayed up nights wondering how I could help a struggling employee turn the corner.

You're going to have days like these, too. Your plan will inspire you when it feels like hope is slipping away.

Resiliency is born out of those moments when you say, "I trust my plan more than I fear any negative results." This kind of faith will make you unstoppable. I should know: my plan took me from one of California's worst neighborhoods to a 6,000 square foot home. When the market crashed and my world was turned upside down, my new plan helped us become the third largest real estate brokerage in Southern California.

Once your plan is formulated, it's time to take massive, inspired action.

*Principle Four*

# TAKE MASSIVE, INSPIRED ACTION

· · · · · · · ·

You see all sorts of characters when you regularly visit the same gym. There's Selfie Guy, who posts two pictures to Instagram for every bicep curl he does. Loud Grunt Gal would make tennis players blush with the primal screams that accompany her lifts.

Right now, you may be picturing a couple of characters who make your workouts more entertaining. But there's another type of person we also see at our local gyms.

These "workout warriors" bear the hallmarks of someone dedicated to fitness: they show up at the same time every day, rocking their name brand outfits and jamming to a playlist spilling out of their headphones. Yet when they actually begin their workout, there's no sweating or grunting. In fact, there are no signs at all that they're pushing themselves further than they went last time they were in the gym.

They're essentially going through the motions, and as a result, their bodies don't change. Peel away the good-looking facade and you're left with a hollow core where their desire and passion should be. For all their efforts, they're not making any progress.

We're all going to take action in our lives. It's the philosophy behind our actions and the intensity with which we undertake them that determine whether those actions bear fruit. The disinterested gym rat is one example of a person whose actions lack the necessary ingredients for success. For some of you, this message might strike a personal chord.

Maybe you're like Travis was at Target: you're unhappy with your job and feel like you're going through the motions. As you look back to when you started that job, you remember being excited, passionate, and seeking unique ways to contribute. You were thrilled by the new opportunities and growing within the company.

Yet your current reality is that you approach every day with diminished intensity. It feels like you're just showing up to get the job done before heading home.

Where action once propelled you forward, now you're running in place. If that's your situation, the time has come for you to take massive, inspired action (MIA).

## FUEL FOR YOUR SOUL

We've spent the first three chapters building up to this moment. It started with living by faith instead of fear to achieve our ideal future. Once we got crystal clear with what we wanted, we made a plan to begin moving forward. Nobody can take action until they've changed their mindset and decided what they want. Now that we've done both, it's time to attack our plan by taking MIA.

MIA is not about making small changes. As the name implies, *massive, inspired action* is life altering. When you feel like it's time to go home, that's when you stay and put in another two hours. This might seem extreme, but remember that achieving something you never thought possible means working harder than you ever imagined you could.

The *inspired* part of MIA means you're driven by something greater than just doing a job. You have to be inspired by the initial vision you set forth for your job, marriage, new business, or life overall. That vision must fuel your actions.

When you take inspired action, no one can get in your way, and no rejection will slow you down or make you feel bad about yourself. You're protected from negative influences, because you're focused on making that vision into your reality.

Once you're ready for MIA, the key is to go all-out for ninety days and have faith in yourself, your vision, and your plan. I mention that time frame because it's typically ninety days' worth of consistent, committed action before your efforts bear fruit, and this is where a lot of entrepreneurs fail. As an employee, these people were accustomed to their efforts leading to a paycheck and seeing immediate rewards for the time they invested. As an entrepreneur, results take time and momentum to develop.

Consistent action is the key to a ninety-day plan. When I say consistent, I mean every workday, be that five days a week or seven. Consistent action builds momentum that will result in an avalanche of new business, even if it's in the final week of those ninety days.

The payoff here isn't so immediate. If you stay committed to your plan and focused on what you want, your actions will bear fruit. But that reward comes in time, which means things may get worse before they get better. Most entrepreneurs aren't built to weather that storm, so they bail and retreat back to the safety of a consistent paycheck.

Even worse are the self-employed among us who make it through the first ninety days—or however long the start-up phase is—intact and then stall out once their initial burst of motivation fades away. With no accountability, these once-hungry entrepreneurs begin to stagnate and blindly follow the same routine, which is a recipe for disaster.

No matter what kind of vision you're trying to actualize in your life, MIA will get you there once you accept the fact that results—higher income, more free time, better relationships, healthier lifestyle—come once you build momentum and that those results might not happen right away.

Results aren't bought with excuses; they require time and consistent effort. That's the *action* part of MIA: doing the same thing over and over without fail. There's nothing sadder than seeing someone fail because they lost their passion. There's no telling how many programmers gave up a few lines of code short of inventing Facebook.

I want you to be Mark Zuckerberg, and you can't do that without the three ingredients of MIA. When you aim for life-altering changes, possess a motivation that reaches deeper than day-to-day work duties, and consistently hone your craft without expecting immediate results, you're going to be successful, no matter what your goals.

That blueprint got me where I am today, so I know for a fact it will work for you.

### THE HARD TRUTH

All that said: MIA is difficult, which means it's not for everyone.

I believe that to be true now more than ever, for the simple reason that we as a country have become soft. We're not as tough as we used to be. Think back sixty years ago to the work ethic our parents and grandparents had to possess to make a living for themselves and their families. There was no Internet, phones were chained to the wall and rotary dial, transportation was slower, and most people had to work every day to survive.

There was no room for any sort of weakness. You were forced to wake up early and do what you had to do, whereas in today's society, we have so many options that were unimaginable in those days. These options allow you to leverage yourself in a variety of ways but can also overwhelm and prevent you from doing things you want to do.

Like every chapter in this book, resiliency is the lifeblood of MIA. When you begin attacking your plan, resiliency makes you strong enough to tough it out, to work a little bit harder, and to deal with rejection. You don't see the mountain in your way, because your path forward takes you right through it, and everything you want is on the other side.

When you have that kind of mind-set, tough times don't even register in your mind. You hit bumps in the road and keep on driving. If you get a flat tire, you pull out the spare.

MIA is not only difficult, but a little scary at times. These are huge changes you're making happen in your life. The stakes are high and you're pouring everything you have into seeing your plan succeed, so it's natural to feel that fear creep in from time to time. You fear failure, rejection, or stopping just short of your goal.

But we know better, don't we? Faith instead of fear now rules our lives, so these scary moments pass quickly, without knocking us off course.

We might be a country of soft excuse makers and feet draggers, but those among us who are ready and willing to take MIA will find an extra dose of resiliency in the most unlikely of places. We just have to be willing to find it.

## WHAT TO DO WHEN THE FIRE IS NOT LIT

A friend of mine came to me one day and said he had started a housecleaning business. It's funny, because in the moment he told me, I thought to myself, "You are not a housecleaning kind of guy. You just don't strike me as that type."

Fast forward a year, and my friend is out of business and has lost a lot of money. He leveraged his home and did it all to keep the business afloat, so he obviously wanted it to work, but the reality is that he wasn't passionate about cleaning houses.

When I asked him about it, he said, "My biggest mistake happened at franchise orientation. When the instructor was saying what my typical day would look like, I had this feeling in the pit of my stomach that told me I didn't really want to do that. Right then, I should've said no and gotten out. But I stayed, and that feeling never went away."

I'll tell you now what I wish I could've told my friend after his orientation: if you're taking MIA and don't feel passionate during the first six to twelve months, you've got problems. When you're first starting on your journey, you should feel the most energized and excited. Passion should be easy to come by.

If you don't feel this passion, there might be a problem with your initial vision. Ask yourself if your end goal is truly something you can't live without. You should desire that outcome so badly you can't live without it, so deeply that *want* becomes *need*. A dying man in the desert doesn't want water: he needs it. Without it, his life is over. Although your vision shouldn't be at the do-or-die level, it should be pretty darn close.

If you can't honestly say your desire is that intense, there's no shame in going back to revise your vision. Better now than after your business fails because you ignored that feeling in your gut that said, "You really don't want to do this. Trust me."

When it comes to waning desire, I think negative influences inside our circle of friends and family are a bigger culprit than we realize. We talked in the first chapter about recognizing good and bad influences in our lives, and I want to revisit that idea for a moment, to discuss the effect our loved ones have on our success.

Sometimes those closest to us can unintentionally cause us harm. For example, my youngest son hadn't scored a goal the entire soccer season, and his team was about to play the final game. Before the game, I said to him, "Visualize yourself scoring the goal. Can you see yourself doing that?" He told me, "Yeah, Dad, I can see it. I can see it."

Without even realizing it, my oldest son said, "You're not going to score a goal, who are you kidding?" I had to stop him right away and address why he was bringing that negativity into our household. I told him, "If you want to be negative, you be negative for yourself. Don't pass that on to other people, especially your younger brother."

How many people do we have in our lives like that? Sometimes they're our closest friends, and other times they're family members. They all mean well, but because of their failures, the injuries they've sustained in their souls and in their hearts, and all the letdowns they've experienced, they try to throw that negativity on you. They approach your situation with their mind-set, and sometimes those comments threaten to derail our motivation, because the person saying them clearly cares about us and our success.

So, I would advise you to be selective with whose input you value as you begin taking MIA. Bad influences can rob joy just as quickly as lackluster vision. If you're struggling with a fire that's not lit, I'd start by looking in those two places.

## TAKING A LOOK IN THE MIRROR

If everyone in the world wholeheartedly believed they could change their lives for the better, do you think there would be people who still chose to settle for mediocrity?

I don't. Nobody would willingly opt for a subpar life with a superior option available.

Ultimately the people who think they can change their world go out and fight for it. Those who don't simply lack the self-belief needed to instigate such change. When you realize that truth, it becomes a matter of looking at the different reasons people lack belief. Sometimes it's as simple as past failures. Other people have negativity ingrained in their minds because they grew up with parents whose default setting was pessimism.

Then there are those who let their circumstances dictate what's possible for their lives. Case in point: my friend Jennifer, who had been in real estate for over a year when she came to me for coaching. We were all excited about Jennifer when she started with our company because of her passion. She seemed like a lock for rookie of the year, with a goal to sell twenty homes in her first year. You couldn't curb her enthusiasm.

The only problem? After a year, instead of selling twenty homes, she had only sold two.

Because I work with my agents on a daily basis and can usually decipher what's going on with people, I knew why she was struggling before she ever came to me. I was ready when she asked me in that first meeting, "Why I am not seeing success?"

"Want to know the truth?" I probed, trying to gauge how prepared she was for an answer I knew she wouldn't enjoy hearing. She said she did, so I took a deep breath and told her, "You're not seeing success because you don't have to succeed."

"What do you mean? Of course I have to succeed!" came her retort.

I expected this response. Again, I don't think anybody willingly shuns a better life, but there are forces we become blind to that can silently suppress our desires. I had pinpointed Jennifer's issue months before and readied myself to deliver some hard truths.

"Let me prove it to you," I told her. "Where do you live right now?"

Slightly offended, she shot back, "What does that have to do with it?"

"It does, just trust me. Tell me where you live."

"I live with my mom."

"OK, and how old are you?"

"I'm twenty-six years old."

A red tinge crept across her face. I could almost feel her embarrassment rising as she stared at the floor. With as much empathy as I could muster, I asked her, "At what point are you planning to move out, get your own place, and start your own life?"

Jennifer remained quiet, turning over my question in her mind. It's likely she had never considered that her dependency on her mom was inhibiting her ability to grow. But I knew that dependency was responsible for her miserable year in real estate, and, as harsh as it might seem, as her coach, I had to help her see the truth that was right in front of her. Without this aha moment, she was in for another disappointing year.

Jennifer's case is not unique. A lot of people lean on spouses, family members, or other loved ones to pay the bills for them and put a roof over their heads. New data shows that young adults ages eighteen to thirty-five are now more likely to live with their parents than with a partner. It's the first time in 130 years that this has been true. Jennifer and millions of others like her suffer from a lack of motivation because they don't *have* to do anything.

Sure, they can go out and try to make a living. But if they have a bad year and don't make the money they need to survive, no worries: Mom and Dad will take care of them.

This dependency goes both ways, mind you. Think about technology with older people. When you talk to them about the newest social media platform or the hottest app, they dismiss you with a wave and some comment like, "My son or daughter does that stuff for me." They don't have to learn about technology, because someone handles it for them.

But what happens if this older person owns a business in a competitive market? The reality is that nowadays you've got to know some basic things about technology when you own a business. You must be able to send an e-mail, create a social media post, and build a simple website. If you remain in the dark because someone else handles "technology stuff" for you, what happens when that person leaves to take another job?

I'll tell you what happens: you lose customers and your business suffers.

We all must be conscious of how we depend on people and make changes when that dependence hinders our ability to grow in necessary and important areas of our lives.

I didn't know it at the time, but I received a gift at age thirteen when my dad became a nonfactor in my life. With the "man of the house" out of the picture, I had no choice but to figure things out on my own. Did it suck? Absolutely. I had no one to go to for advice, no safety net for tough times. My family depended on me, not the other way around.

I had to grow up way faster than any teenager should, but I'm grateful for that growth, despite the rough patches that inevitably came with no father around. After all, I grew into a young man who made six figures two years after graduating high school, owned a home by age twenty-one, and made a million bucks a year by age twenty-six.

Does any of that happen if I'm still living my comfortable life in New York with all the privileges of wealth and both parents around? Maybe, but I doubt it. The biggest reason for my success was simply having no other choice. I was either going to figure out how to thrive or suffer a life of mediocrity. Unlike some, I never lacked the self-belief needed to seize my higher calling. I envisioned my success and pursued it relentlessly.

Jennifer lacked belief in herself and didn't even know it. By living with her mom at age twenty-six, she was inadvertently admitting she wasn't willing to bet on her own success. She might have struggled with this revelation at first, but she quickly realized the truth of what I was telling her. It was the "cold water" moment she needed to shake her out of apathy.

I'm happy to report that, after our meeting, Jennifer has rebounded beautifully and is on track to sell between six and ten homes this year. She's not quite ready to reach her initial goal of twenty closings in a year, but she's well on her way to that kind of success.

## THE ANSWER IS ALWAYS WITHIN

Part of the reason my business is so successful is because I teach people like Jennifer how to overcome obstacles unrelated to real estate and help them become better people in the process. Yet, when you think about it, who the heck taught me that? If a teacher must first be a student, how did a fatherless kid in a California slum become a business owner and mentor before his fortieth birthday? It doesn't seem to add up.

Well, that fatherless kid was hungry enough to find a solution to any problem he faced. He realized that nobody was going to give him anything, and the only way he was going to improve his life was by educating himself. He went to the ends of the earth to find the people, resources, seminars, trainings, and books he needed to fulfill the vision for who he wanted to become. He knew his parents weren't going to take care of him, so he developed a hunger for information, which propelled him to unimaginable success.

I don't have all the answers, but I do have this simple truth: the answer is always within.

Whenever I sit down to coach someone, I start with the knowledge that the solution to their problem can be found inside themselves. I'm not going to provide that answer, and neither is my company. The questions I ask my agents begin the process of inward reflection and help them identify the root cause of their issues. Once we have that information, we design a plan and see how they can take MIA.

Being self-reliant can help you in any situation, even if it's bowling with friends on a Friday night. I was in that situation recently, and as I sat there tugging on those god-awful clown shoes they make you wear, my competitive fire was being stoked.

It didn't matter that I'd been bowling only once or twice in my life, I still expected to top the scores of my fellow bowlers. I want to win whether you're friend or foe, professional or amateur. (I realize this might be unhealthy, but I know some of you can relate.)

My first game was less than ideal. The ball went in the gutter, hit one pin, and generally did everything it's not supposed to do. After a few frames, I had a choice to make. I could continue stinking up the joint and leave that night knowing I got my butt kicked—I'd rather walk on hot coals—or I could fix the problem.

Of course, I picked the second option. So I asked myself, "How can I become a better bowler literally right now?" If the answer is always within, I knew there was a way.

My lightbulb moment was to Google "bowling for dummies." I quickly learned that I wasn't bowling well was because I was releasing the ball too high and my wrist wasn't locked. Those two minor changes made all the difference. I was picking up strikes and spares in no time because I believed the answer was out there for me to find.

I didn't win at bowling that night, but I came in third place out of seven. Give me three more cracks at it and I guarantee you I'll win. (Like I said: plenty of self-confidence!)

You have the ability to find the answers you seek. If you don't want to suffer through another year of selling only two homes, how are you going to change that outcome? If you want to own a home by age twenty-one, what does it take to make that purchase?

*What are you going to do about it?*

That's a very simple question people don't ask themselves. Those who do discover a whole wellspring of passion and resiliency they might not have known about.

As an eighteen-year-old living in a bad neighborhood, I knew I didn't want my seven-year-old brother going through what I went through. That's all I knew. I didn't know anything about real estate, or building a business, or mentoring others. The *how* isn't important at first. Don't worry about how it's going to happen, just get crystal clear with what you want and then follow the steps we're outlining in this book. You'll find the *how* as you go.

I certainly didn't know how things would turn out at age sixteen, when I was buying courses from these crazy infomercial guys, ones that I had no business buying, and just devouring the information. I was so hungry to learn and I knew exactly what I wanted, so if the crazy infomercial guys could help, I'd give them a shot. (Shocker: they didn't help!)

I wish I could say the same for Edward, my friend from high school who had tons of ambition and a great work ethic. He just had no direction or goal he was pursuing. Like a lot of people, Edward would do just about anything to make a buck. We both had our real estate licenses right out of high school, and when the broker we were working for offered him $100 to wash and wax his brand new 7 Series BMW, Edward was ecstatic.

Even though I was broke and needed the money, I can vividly remember what I told Edward when he asked me if I wanted to help him clean the BMW.

"I don't want to wax that BMW," I said. "I want to own one someday."

## EDDIE FINDS HIS SUCCESS

I want to end this chapter with a story about my friend Eddie (not to be confused with Edward), who is my partner in my real estate investing firm. His job is straightforward, to manage our process, which is simple: buy properties, remodel them, and sell them for a large profit. During his first year as an investor, Eddie was like the guy we talked about who was going to the gym and not working out with full intensity. Half the time when I'd walk by his office, he'd be in there asleep.

Nevertheless, Eddie would come into work every day and repeat this process. Honestly, it was hard to watch. It wasn't until one day when Eddie was about to get married that he realized how badly he'd been wasting his time and energy. A bit panicked, he came to me and said, "I'm ready to do whatever it takes. Show me what to do, and I'll do it."

I gave him an outline to follow, and he spent the next ninety days working from 8:00 a.m. to 8:00 p.m. Taking MIA wasn't easy for Eddie. He came to me on day sixty saying he wanted to quit and he didn't think he could make it. I always had to remind him that this process took ninety days, and he had to remain committed. To his credit, he never quit.

After those ninety days, he saw zero results.

I wasn't worried, though. During that day-sixty meltdown, I asked Eddie a question I ask a lot of my agents during coaching sessions. "Eddie," I said, looking him in the eye, "can you honestly tell me that you are working your absolute hardest, that you are focused and energized, and that you are attacking your plan on a daily basis?"

When I ask this question, the answer is no 90 percent of the time. However, in Eddie's case, I knew the answer was yes, because my office was next to his and I could see him doing it. He answered, "Yes, I can honestly say that."

I told him, "Then you have nothing to worry about. You're attached to the results, but I want you to be attached to the fact that this has been the best sixty days of consistent hard work in your life. You should be proud of yourself for that, and I promise you that if you can just keep going for another thirty days, you will see those deals start coming in."

In days 91 through 120, Eddie bought eight houses.

Within a thirty-day span, he equaled the number of homes he had bought in the previous year. Today, as I write this book—and I know you may not believe this—we are on track to buy and sell eighty homes this year! Eddie did this by taking MIA and hanging in through the good and bad.

He attached himself to the process and not the results, and, with that simple mind-set shift, he accomplished more in thirty days than he had in his entire career. He took the ninety-day cycle literally and hasn't stopped. He's now onto his second ninety-day cycle and is getting massive results.

This book's first three chapters laid the groundwork for your success, and MIA is the fuel you need to reach your desired outcome. MIA transforms the way you work, provides motivation when the results don't happen instantly, and keeps you pounding away when everything and everyone says to give up.

This process won't feel like work, because you've never worked like this before in your life. Once you're on the other side of your start-up phase and begin seeing results, you'll look back and marvel at how, when you're motivated and making big changes in your life, the days fly by. You'll recall those long days and think, "Man, that was fun!"

Your first taste of success can't make you complacent, though. Sustained excellence is what we're after, and that doesn't happen unless you track your numbers.

*Principle Five*

# TRACK YOUR NUMBERS

. . . . . . .

I knew from the minute I saw the numbers that something was wrong.

Here we were in middle of home-buying season and our number of homes sold each month was trending...downward? My heart was in my throat as I studied the charts:

- March 2016: sold 289 homes
- April 2016: sold 265 homes
- May 2016: sold 255 homes
- June 2016: sold 215 homes

What was causing this regression? I noticed the trend in May and thought we might rebound in June, but we didn't. We were in bad shape and, if things didn't turn around, we'd be in danger of missing our goal of doing a billion dollars in sales in 2016.

I became like a doctor at that point, analyzing every part of our business to see what was working and what wasn't. Were we not helping our agents grow? I checked in on our classes, and they were still doing a phenomenal job teaching agents. We had people breaking through every day thanks to those classes, so that wasn't the issue.

Was there something wrong with the market? I pulled up the market report and analyzed the data. Strike two: our market was actually up compared with this time last year.

One by one, I was eliminating possible problems, which was good. The downside was that I hadn't yet found the cause of our sales downturn. I decided to look at our approach to see if our team was doing anything differently in June compared with March.

Bingo! The answer nearly jumped off the page at me. I got to work right away making adjustments to fix the problem and get our company back on track. We'll cover the specific issue and the adjustments I made in chapter 6, but if I hadn't been tracking our numbers, I wouldn't have had any idea we were off track or known how to fix it.

Once you start implementing the various phases of your plan, you can't move forward unless you're tracking your numbers. Without knowing where you've been, what's working, and what's not working, you can't plot a course forward for your business.

## THE THREE PERSONALITY TYPES IN BUSINESS

Before we dig into why tracking is important, let's look at the three personality types in business and the differences in how each type approaches numbers.

The first personality type is a skilled producer. This is someone with a unique skill who produces results using that skill on a daily basis, whether it be cooking, public speaking, cleaning teeth, selling homes as a real estate agent. No matter the skill, they're using it to generate a lot of business, which is nice in the short term.

But, as we'll see, the difference between generating a lot of new business and doing continuous business with repeat customers comes down to tracking your numbers.

The second personality type is an organization manager, someone with a knack for leading groups of people. We all know someone who fits this personality type. Assuming they're in the right role, CFOs, CEOs, and other three-letter jobs fall into this category.

The third type of business personality is the entrepreneur, whose main focus is making a profit. If you're an entrepreneur or know one, you understand the struggle of filling multiple roles in your business to keep it afloat until you can hire more people or leverage yourself through marketing and advertising.

Which of those personality types would you guess has the hardest time tracking their numbers? The entrepreneur working fourteen-hour days to keep their business alive might seem like the right answer, but it's the skilled producer who actually struggles most.

Here's why: when skilled producers do what they do best, they generate a ton of business and make a lot of money. But just because someone can captivate an audience while they're onstage, or make your teeth shine bright white, doesn't mean they understand what it takes to run a business. Skilled producers are masters of their domain. Running a business, however, requires a different kind of expertise.

Organization managers get where they are by being detail-oriented people capable of seeing the big picture. Their ability to lead others depends on a micro viewpoint, and their ability to lead a company depends on a macro viewpoint, which includes where they want the company to go. Without numbers, they can't perform either task.

Entrepreneurs, if they're serious about being successful, live and die by their numbers. When you're first starting out and spending your own money or investor capital, you will pinch every penny and track every dollar you spend. I've been there before with businesses I've started and learned the hard way that the numbers are your lifeline.

If you're a skilled producer, don't be bummed out thinking you can't become a master of numbers. You absolutely can! I should know: I'm a skilled producer who looks at my company's numbers every single day. When you make something a priority in your life, you can turn any deficiency into a strength. We'll talk about this more in a moment.

We were in business six years before I finally pulled the trigger and hired a COO. Having a COO has allowed me the freedom to develop new strategies to grow our company still more. All businesses need an organization manager to help the visionary implement the vision they have for the business.

Whether it's you or a COO, you must track your numbers if you want to be successful.

## IF YOU DON'T KNOW THE NUMBERS, YOU'RE FLYING BLIND

The way to grow a business is not by emotion, not by a feeling, and not by skill. Year-on-year growth happens when you look at your numbers and understand the story they're telling you. Business is data driven. If you don't have the numbers and don't know the story, you're flying blind at the controls of an emotion-driven business.

Can you fly blind and do well for a while? Sure. But you'll never be able to duplicate yourself or create something enormous without understanding your numbers.

Tracking is important regardless of the industry you're in, because numbers show you where you're efficient and where you're lacking. Every action you take leads to victory or failure. If you don't know what's going right and what's going wrong, whether your actions are resulting in growth or stagnation, you might repeat mistakes that sabotage the future of your business.

I'll use myself as an example. The business I had in 2008, right before the market crashed, was doing really well.

Little did I know we were headed for trouble, because I wasn't tracking my numbers. I didn't even know my business personality type.

I'm a skilled producer to my core. While I was working in that business, I never put on my entrepreneur or organization manager hat to look at our numbers, nor did I delegate that task to somebody who was better suited for the role. We were generating new business and making money, so I kept doing what I'd always done.

Like a pilot flying without his gauges, we were headed for disaster. The failure of that business, and where my family ended up as a result, is the reason I'm so passionate about tracking my numbers. I've seen firsthand what happens when you don't, and the results aren't pretty. Don't let success spoil you: track your numbers.

Before we identify some specific numbers you should know, let's walk through the process of how businesses attract new customers and nurture those relationships.

## FROM CONTACT TO REPEAT CUSTOMER

A contact is the first rung in the business-transaction ladder. I use this broad term to describe everyone who is exposed to your business in some form or fashion: talking with you, walking past your location, receiving direct-mail marketing, and so on. You cast a wide net and try to get as many eyeballs on your business as possible.

The next rung on the ladder is what every business covets—a lead, or someone who has expressed an interest in what you have to offer. Professionals in many industries, especially real estate, depend on leads. Each one is a golden ticket.

Of course, a golden ticket is only useful if you do something with it. When you have a lead, you need to create an opportunity to earn their business. In real estate, we set appointments and make presentations to try to persuade buyers or sellers to work with us as agents. If you're a car dealership, you want to get leads on the lot to show them cars and convince them they'd be crazy not to purchase a new vehicle.

Whatever your industry, your business will live or die with lead conversion. If you're throwing away golden tickets and not advancing leads to the next stage, your time in business will be short-lived. Such a pronouncement sounds harsh, but it's true.

You don't need to be a salesperson to get results when meeting with leads. If you're passionate about your business, you're perfectly equipped to sell it. As long as you don't come unprepared or insult someone during the appointment, passion is often enough to get the deal done. Excitement and energy are contagious in these meetings, and if you make the lead feel the passion you have, you have a great shot at getting a sale.

A sale is the result of all the work you've done up to this point. It's gliding into the end zone after a long touchdown run. You nailed the presentation, and your lead is now a customer. Congratulations! Speaking from experience, there's nothing better than filling the need your customer has and impacting your business financially at the same time.

A sale seems like victory, but it's not the end of the road. Most people really mess things up for their businesses by thinking that everything stops after the sale. In reality, everything starts after the sale is complete.

Attracting new customers is nice, but we're more concerned about how many of those customers come back and buy from us again. How many repeat customers are we creating, and what's the frequency with which they're coming back to buy again?

Remember: new customers grow your business.

Repeat customers sustain your business.

## THE NUMBERS THAT TELL THE STORY

Within the "contact-to-repeat-customer" process, you probably see some metrics you need to track. Starting from the beginning: How many contacts are you reaching? What's it costing to reach those people? Could you do a better job reaching them?

Envision your ideal customer and think about where they spend their time, how they consume new information, and what channels they use to discover new products.

If you're not seeing a high percentage of contacts becoming leads, you might be fishing in the wrong pond, or you might be fishing with the wrong bait. If you think newspaper ads aren't working, switch to online advertising and track those results. If you think you're in the right place, switch up your message and monitor the response you get.

The key to turning contacts into leads is testing everything, finding what works, and pouring your resources into that approach. You're going to fail during the initial phase, when you're trying to build a customer base. The key is to fail quickly and cheaply, learn what went wrong, and pivot to something else that's supported by your findings.

Once you attain the contact-to-lead conversion percentage you need, the next step is to track how many appointments you schedule with those leads. Getting belly to belly with that golden ticket lets you show them your product or service can solve their problem.

If they're a hot lead—someone who is ready to buy right now—they might not need any convincing. You need to get in front of warm leads, those people who know they have a problem but need to be convinced that your business can provide the solution. Cold leads are those people who don't even know they have a problem yet. Most of them will need to be warmed up before they're ready to meet with you and discuss a solution.

Assuming you're attracting the right kind of leads and identifying how close they are to making a purchase, you should be booking plenty of appointments. If you're struggling to get in front of leads, you need to change your approach. Don't assume there's something wrong with the leads you're getting and continue going about things the same way.

The key, once you get in front of leads, is, of course, efficiency. I see this every day with the real estate agents I coach. If you're meeting with ten people but only signing three contracts, what does that say? I can think of a few explanations.

It might indicate a problem with your lead segmentation. You might think you're meeting with warm leads, when in reality you're meeting with cold leads. If that's the case, you need to generate new ideas for qualifying and segmenting your leads so that you're not wasting your time with appointments that likely won't go in your favor.

A low conversion rate could also be the result of a lackluster presentation. Appointments let you emotionally connect with people as you're telling them about your business. Remember: people buy with emotion and justify with logic. Inject some personal stories or testimonials into your presentation if it needs more emotional resonance.

Finally, you might just be afraid to close. When it comes time to put a pen in their hand, so to speak, you can't let low self-confidence keep you from closing the deal. Trust your gut. If you know someone is ready to purchase, don't be the reason they walk out of your store without your product in hand. Keep notes on how you handle different situations at the finish line and share them with your team so they can learn from your experience.

You won't convince every lead, but if your process is sound, you should be converting leads into customers at a rate higher than the average in your industry.

Yes, I said *higher* than the industry average. If you're not at that point yet, keep refining how you handle leads until you're the gold standard in your industry.

If businesses live or die with lead conversion, don't settle for just living. Thrive!

When you get into the customer side of things and start talking about sales, you want to consider your average revenue per sale. Income is nice, especially if you're selling something like homes or cars, but revenue is the true indicator of success.

You might have made $1,000 on your sale, but how much did it take to acquire that lead and move them along the path to becoming a customer? What did the product cost? If you paid $300 to acquire the product, and you spent another $150 getting it in the customer's hands, your revenue for that sale is $550. Look at each product you're selling, add up all the revenue on sales of that product, and divide it by the number of customers who purchased it. There's your average revenue per sale.

Is that dollar amount what you need to grow your business? If it's not enough, you have to figure out ways to improve your process and raise your bottom line.

Make sure you're tracking how many repeat customers you get. How often do those customers come back and how much are they spending each time?

Devote some extra time, effort, and money to keeping repeat customers happy. They are your brand ambassadors, the people who'll rave about your business to others, and they're more effective than any advertising campaign you could run.

When you're tracking numbers like new customers, repeat customers, and average revenue per sale—among many others—you can begin to extrapolate growth and set some future baselines. If the numbers are saying you should sell 150 cars next month, and you're at fifty cars halfway through the month, you'll know something is wrong in your business and can begin diagnosing possible issues.

We'll cover the types of adjustments you can make in chapter 6, but for now, I hope you can see that numbers give you ultimate control over your future success.

## UNDERSTAND WHERE YOUR MONEY IS GOING

You can't run a successful business if you don't know your costs. This sounds obvious, doesn't it? How can you expect to make money if you don't know what you're spending to generate new business? What if you're losing money each time you make a sale?

You'd be amazed how many people I know or I've worked with who can't seem to grasp this fundamental concept. It doesn't matter how many fish you're bringing into the boat if that boat is taking on water. You're still going to sink and lose everything!

We'll talk later in this chapter about why people don't track their numbers, but regardless of how you feel about budgets and number crunching, I hope you understand how crucial it is to track your spending. If you're not already doing this in your personal life or in your business, you need to start *right now*. Your future success depends on it.

When we're talking about improving our bottom line by changing our process, there are two basic places we can look: cost of goods sold and cost of acquiring leads.

The cost of goods sold is what you're out of pocket before you even begin. Let's say you're a Realtor and you make an agreement with a builder for a 3 percent commission, with the caveat that you pay a 20 percent referral fee for every sale you get from the builder. Right off the bat, every sale is costing you 20 percent of your commission check.

If you're selling a plate of food, or a phone, or a boat, what do you pay to acquire that product and sell it? If your revenue is not where you want it to be, do you need to consider selling a different product or looking for a different distributor?

My personal philosophy is that you never sacrifice quality for the sake of reducing your costs. Trying to cut corners will ultimately drive customers away.

On the customer side, look at your marketing or advertising budget for the past month. How much did you spend on acquiring leads? How many leads did you get during that month? Every industry is different, but there's always a price point at which you know your cost per conversion—the cost of turning a contact into a lead—is too high.

Once you have that lead, how much are you paying the employees who convert those leads into customers? What does it cost to keep your workplace open and give your team a place to work? Do they need expensive equipment? Are you in an industry where it's customary to leave behind materials after a presentation? There are many hidden costs of doing business, and you need to track them all.

What you can't do is inflict unnecessary costs on yourself. I see this all the time in real estate, where agents will give the house away because they feel like they're not worth the commission they should be earning. They'll give discounts because they don't feel like they're offering value that justifies the commission.

It's mind-boggling to me that agents do this to themselves. Value yourself and the services you're offering, because if you don't, the customer certainly won't! Can you imagine a world in which Apple would discount their fees? It would never happen.

Be like Apple; know your worth and stand by it. Don't burden yourself with extra cost. Go out there and deliver service that makes customers think, "I got a heck of a deal!"

## WHY YOU'RE NOT TRACKING YOUR NUMBERS (AND WHAT TO DO ABOUT IT)

Being in business is not for the faint of heart.

No business in history has enjoyed a smooth ride to the top of its industry with zero bumps in the road. Periods of success will be followed by challenging times that will test your commitment to your business and your perseverance.

Companies like Apple, Nike, and McDonald's didn't get to where they are by how they handled success, but rather by how they dealt with failure.

You might be terrified of failure, of working for years to build your business, only to see it crumble and fade away. If so, you're not alone. The fear of failure is a powerful motivator that drives countless entrepreneurs to work harder than everybody else.

You've read in this book about my failures in business, and how they nearly destroyed my confidence. I had to hit rock bottom, on that day when our air conditioner broke, to snap out of my funk and get back to work. If you're haunted by past failures and lacking confidence right now, I completely understand what you're going through.

Past failures and the fear of failure are powerful enough to keep people from looking at their numbers, because they're afraid of the story they'll see. They prefer the warm and fuzzy approach of running their business based on emotion, because it doesn't include the "splash of cold water" shock their numbers might give them.

What if they open their books and see that they're losing money? What if they're already in debt and have to fire employees to salvage the business? A blow like that would crush their confidence and their egos. They're not ready to accept any unpleasant truths their numbers would reveal and prefer to stay in the fantasy world they've created until the "out of business" sign is hanging on the front door.

I have one piece of advice for those in business who, for whatever reason, refuse to look at their numbers: get out of business. You're not going to make it.

I know this sounds harsh, but it's more pleasant than losing your business. Trust me, I know that feeling. You have to be stronger than the personal issues and past experiences that are holding you back. If not for you, then for your employees. If not for your employees, then for your customers. If not for your customers, then for your stakeholders. If not for your stakeholders, then for the people who depend on you.

I conquered my personal struggles for my family. If you need a source of inspiration that will never falter, I know of none better than persevering for your family.

If this section is speaking to your soul, I don't just want to give you a wake-up call. This book is all about solutions, so let's look at how to conquer this challenge and arrive at a place where you're confident and committed to tracking your numbers.

You start by identifying your deficiencies. As much as we don't like to think about it, we all have areas of weakness. In business, you have to analyze those weaknesses and turn them into areas of strength. Although this might sound impossible, depending on your deficiencies, I promise that real change can happen as long as you're determined.

Some of you might be struggling with a mind-set issue that is causing you take the wrong approach and sabotage your success. One easy way to correct a mind-set issue is by reading books or listening to podcasts by thought leaders like Tony Robbins or Robert Kiyosaki. You might also consider coaching from someone who has enjoyed success in your industry. I say that not only as a coach myself, but as someone who personally knows the impact that coaching can have when a career is stuck in neutral.

Perhaps your deficiency is a belief issue that keeps you from reaching out and seizing the success right in front of you. We touched on this briefly with salespeople who are afraid to close, but a belief issue can go deeper than that. A deficient belief system can cause you to accept any number of lies about your business:

- We've hit our ceiling and don't have what it takes to grow past this point.

- We're not prepared to take on a job this big. What if we fall on our face?
- Every business struggles to get new customers. We're fine.
- I'm unhappy in my own business, but this is the life I've chosen.

Don't believe these lies for one second.

If you've worked through this book chapter by chapter, you know we kicked a weak belief system to the curb in chapters 1 and 2. If you're still struggling or just started reading with this chapter, go back and study those chapters. You'll clear your head of lies like these and restore your belief in yourself and your business.

We as humans deal with a lot of issues that could lead to the demise of our businesses. That's the reality of the situation, but the truth is that we don't have to let our issues hold us captive. We have the authority to work on those deficiencies and turn them into strengths, or even delegate to someone already gifted in that area.

I'll use myself as an example. I know that I'm an artist and need a manager to help with the organization aspect of my business. I'm not bad at organization, it's just not my forte. I'd rather use my time and skills to produce results for the company.

Find your deficiencies and ask yourself what you're going to do about them. Once you've grown as a person, and those weaknesses are no longer stumbling blocks, then you're ready to look at the numbers and see the story they're telling. You have to start with self-reflection and self-improvement before you can improve your business.

Your business is a reflection of you as a person. If you're a successful person internally, then your business will be successful. If you're feeling down and out or scared, your business will reflect that feeling. You have to model the characteristics you want people to associate with your business. Bottom line: it all starts with you.

Do you want to take control? Or do you want to get out?

In the world of business, there's no middle ground.

### WHAT HAPPENS WHEN YOU STOP TRACKING

Success has a way of bringing out our worst habits.

We all have a thermometer that measures how close we are to getting what we want. Some thermometers are bigger than others, and some deal with personal goals, whereas others focus on business goals. We might be trying to lose twenty-five pounds or transform our business from a fledgling start-up to an Inc. 5000 company. No matter the goal, we're committed to achieving the milestones along the way.

The minute we start gaining ground on that success threshold and creeping up that thermometer, what tends to happen? We start slowing down, relaxing, and feeling like we've got things figured out. That momentary taste of success turns off the discipline of tracking our numbers and doing the things that brought us early success.

The dieter stops counting each calorie and mixes in a few too many candy bars. The entrepreneur stops going after new business with the same intensity and rests on his laurels, while his competitors snatch away prospective clients.

Early success makes us forget that what got us from point A to point B is not enough to get us to point C and beyond. The most apt metaphor for filling our thermometer is not pushing a stalled car down a hill—it gets easier as you go—but rather climbing Mount Everest. The journey only gets more challenging the longer you go. I'm no mountain-climbing expert, but I'm pretty sure that if you stop climbing, you'll freeze to death.

Consistent number tracking is the acid test for how serious we are about long-term success and the grander vision we have for our life and business. Too many people get bogged down with short-term worries and focus only on paying the bills.

I'm not saying that paying your bills is unimportant. What I am saying is that you can't let the minutiae of life or the taste of early success make you complacent.

I talk with people all the time who tell me their numbers are in their head—which is a steel trap, apparently. Tell me: What did you have for breakfast yesterday? When was the last time you called your mom? What's the last movie you saw?

A flaw of human design is that our memories can be hazy. We misremember things the further removed we are from them. Numbers don't lie. Numbers give you an honest and reliable picture of what's going on, even if you remember it differently.

Relying on your memory to recall specific business metrics is beyond risky. It's reckless. Even if you have a photographic memory and can recall details from years gone by, how are you supposed to analyze that data to look for patterns or trends? A huge part of filling that thermometer involves anticipating shifts in your industry and being prepared.

Technology has changed everything, and only the forward-thinking companies are going to survive. When your numbers start to shift for reasons beyond your control, take a step back and survey the landscape.

Knowing where you fit and how you compare to competitors gives you a fuller picture and will help you make informed decisions as big shifts approach. In between tectonic movements in the marketplace, you should use the numbers at your disposal to make frequent adjustments and keep your business on track.

*Principle Six*

# MAKE ADJUSTMENTS BASED ON THE NUMBERS

· · · · · · ·

Our company's declining sales from March to June 2016 didn't stem from a lack of training for our agents or a slumping market in our area. Our issue was purely psychological.

In March, we sold 289 homes. We'd never done that before, so everyone was fired up and celebrating this great milestone for our company.

The problem was that we didn't handle success very well. The number of vacations shot up in April and our team took its foot off the gas. We thought we'd reached the finish line already and lost that hunger to achieve greater results in the following months. Our agents lived off the glory of that March performance for three months, and our results subsequently tanked, bottoming out with just 215 homes sold in June.

We have since bounced back and now average between 350 and 400 sales a month, but it was a reminder that a strong month followed by a weak month negates the strong month.

The psychological side of business has such a huge impact on performance, yet we often don't think about this at first when our numbers begin to drop. I was guilty of that while diagnosing our problem in June: I looked at external factors like agent training and the market, when the real issue was motivation and drive, two internal factors.

Discovering this helped me realize something that most business owners never understand, yet it is a fundamental part of growing any business: business is 80 percent psychology and 20 percent strategy. I learned this invaluable insight from Tony Robbins, who is a legend in business.

Business owners too often want to diagnose strategy when problems arise. In reality, the strategy piece is only as good as the people you have in place to carry it out. If your employees are miserable, unfulfilled, or ill equipped for their roles, your business will not last. Your physical business can't create lifelong customers; only people can do that.

So how did we fix our slumping sales? We helped our agents return to a peak state where they felt their absolute best. We built them up as people first and agents second. We implemented new training for them and stayed in their ear all day long with more inspirational messages. We got people out of bed earlier and working out more. We focused on improving their health, mind-set, and overall well-being, which increased their joy and empowered them to perform at a high level.

We understand that in a sales organization, your salespeople must feel great. We're not accountants, doctors, or lawyers. Sales is a different beast. Our success depends on energy and enthusiasm. If our agents aren't juiced up when they walk through the door, their customers will pick up on it, and it will probably be a bad sales day.

If you have any doubts that business is psychological, or you think all the "rah rah" stuff doesn't make a difference, I'll let our numbers for July and August prove my point:

- July 2016: sold 286 homes
- August 2016: sold 383 homes

The adjustments we made not only got us back to our previous high within one month, but allowed us to leapfrog that record by almost 100 sales in August.

Being able to react quickly and implement changes in your business begins with having the right culture in place. None of the adjustments we made in July would have been possible without buy-in from our agents. Once we showed them the numbers, and they realized how bad things had gotten, they were onboard to try what we suggested.

If you've done a great job leading your troops, and they know you genuinely care about their well-being, they won't question your intentions. They'll know that all you're trying to do is inspire them and push the organization to accomplish its goals. My team was able to look past my words—no small task, because I was showing them how poorly we'd done—and see that I was trying to motivate them on a personal level.

If you're not at a place with your team where you'd feel comfortable making changes based on your numbers, you have to get there. Not every adjustment will be like the one we made and deal outright with employee psychology, but

I bet that if you dig into any strategy issue your business is having, there's some internal factor at play.

You can't make any kind of adjustment unless your employees trust and respect you. Once they do, you can study the numbers and conquer any obstacle together.

## "I FELT LIKE I'D MADE IT"

I coach a salesman named Adrian, whose business was struggling. According to Adrian, he was working his tail off and yet his business wasn't producing the results he wanted. He came to me eager to identify the problem and willing to make adjustments.

The first thing we did was pull up his numbers. What jumped off the page right away was the number of people entering his store. Or should I say, the number of people not entering his store. On average, 100 people would enter Adrian's store per week. In recent months, that number had dropped as low as twenty per week.

Losing 80 percent of his weekly contacts was such a massive problem that I was surprised Adrian hadn't spotted it already. "What's happening here," I explained to him, "is that you've stopped doing the activities necessary to get people in the door."

"Man, I didn't even realize it," he responded. His expression was pure embarrassment.

I didn't want him to shut down on me, so I said, "Let's talk through this together. What were you doing when you were getting 100 people in the store?"

"I was going out and networking more," he answered. "I mailed out postcards and ran advertisements, basically doing whatever I could to share our services with people."

"What caused you to stop all that?" I asked.

His answer was a revelation.

"To be honest, I felt like I'd made it," he said. "It felt like I'd arrived, like I had achieved all my goals. When that happened, I stopped doing the things that I used to do."

Behind Adrian's strategic problem was an internal issue. He got a taste of early success and mistakenly thought he'd crossed the finish line. He needed to start pushing harder than ever to keep his momentum going, but instead he did the opposite.

I didn't have to design a new training for Adrian or send him inspirational messages throughout the day. We created a ninety-day action plan that got him back to doing the activities that had brought people into the store. Just by admitting his mistake out loud, Adrian was able to identify the root cause of his struggles and move past it.

After ninety days, Adrian had over 100 people coming into the store every week. Not only that, but his sales were up, and he was generating more revenue than ever before.

Adrian's story contains the three essential ingredients for a turnaround:

1. **The numbers:** If you don't track your numbers, you can't know the story of your business. Adrian was smart enough to track his numbers, even if his diminishing motivation and drive kept him from seeing his very obvious problem.
2. **The attitude:** Adrian genuinely wanted to turn things around. When I asked him how important his business was to him, he said, "It's everything to me." Turning things around can be tough. You need to be sure you're up for the challenge.
3. **The adjustment:** Once we restored Adrian's desire to grow his business, I turned him loose with that action plan, and he never looked back.

If your business is struggling today, you can turn things around if you start with your numbers, maintain a positive attitude, and make an appropriate adjustment.

## ACTIVITIES DRIVE RESULTS

Adrian's story illustrates the power of adjusting your activities. Complacency knocked Adrian off track and he stopped networking, marketing, and advertising.

As a business owner, consider the following questions in regard to your activities:

- What are you doing at each level of your business that's getting huge results?
    - → Look at your activities during each step of the transaction process: reaching contacts, generating leads, setting appointments, making sales, and creating repeat customers. What stands out?
    - → Stress the importance of consistently performing these actions.
- What are activities where one small tweak could make a huge difference?
    - → Perhaps you're sending out postcards to contacts, but you're not getting as many leads as you want. Would your contacts respond better to a phone call? Does your postcard copy need updating?
    - → This is more about tightening up your activity than overhauling it.
- Where are some areas where your activities are completely missing the mark?

→ Are you getting a ton of leads in the door but not clos-ing enough sales? You might need better training for your sales team. Is it time to scrap your old market-ing approach and create some content for inbound marketing?

→ You can't hesitate to switch gears if something isn't working. Consider this quote from Marcus Tullius Cicero: "It is the nature of every person to err, but only the fool perseveres in error." Don't play the fool!

- What are some activities you aren't doing that you should consider?

  → Is your business growth stalled because you've never gone to networking events and met other business owners, potential customers, or investors? You'll never know how an activity affects your business until you try it.

  → Consider hiring someone if you don't have time for new activities but want to start implementing them within your business.

If your activities aren't driving results, they're merely wasting your time.

## LOCATION, LOCATION, LOCATION

Another type of adjustment involves your location. A brick-and-mortar restaurant might see sagging numbers because they're located in the back of a warehouse somewhere. They're not getting foot traffic, and people who've eaten there struggle to tell their friends how to get there. The adjustment for that restaurant is simple: find a better location.

There's an old adage that the three most important factors in real estate are "location, location, location." For agents, this goes deeper than what neighborhood their new listing is in, or whether they can find houses to show buyers in a particular part of town.

Location had a big impact on my ability to generate seller leads early in my career. I was knocking on doors in this one neighborhood and had a stretch where I was getting a ton of new leads. Things couldn't have been going better. Then I switched my location. For the next thirty days in the new neighborhood, I didn't generate a single lead.

Because I was using the same approach, I figured the problem had to be my location. Turns out I was knocking on doors in a neighborhood where everybody was a little older and more established. In this neighborhood, people weren't thinking about moving.

Location can factor into the success of a business in ways that aren't obvious. Luxury automobile dealers need to know where their target customers live if they're considering a direct mail campaign. Sending flyers advertising six-figure car brands to a starter neighborhood would be as effective as throwing those flyers in the garbage.

Did you open a cool new bar close to campus in a college town? Seems like a foolproof business plan until you learn you've set up shop next to a suitcase school. You'll have to get creative to give students a reason to stick around when they'd usually head home. Dollar drink nights, anyone?

Some adjustments involving location are easy, such as mailing flyers to the right areas of town. Others are a huge endeavor, like opening a new location for your restaurant.

The best way to avoid location as an issue for your business is to do your research ahead of time and consider all the pros and cons of where you're setting up shop. The more issues you deal with up front, the fewer you'll have to adjust for down the road.

### CAN YOU HEAR ME NOW?

One adjustment that hugely successful businesses are adept at making is improving efficiency, and oftentimes that comes down to communicating more effectively.

Skilled communication serves your business in a couple ways. We never could have implemented the changes we made in July if our company's internal communication was dysfunctional. Large companies have a lot of moving pieces, which means leaders have to be on the same page when they're disseminating new information.

If you aren't doing so already, you should hold regular—at least quarterly—meetings with leaders in your business to discuss improvements that can be made.

If you have good employees who are constantly coming to you asking for information they should already know, you need to adjust how you communicate with them. That could mean holding weekly meetings, moving your team to a platform for workplace communication like Slack, or creating a single point of contact so employees know who to talk with and aren't receiving messages filtered through different leaders.

Uninformed or misinformed employees can have a negative impact on your customer service, which in turn makes your business look bad.

I'm not talking here about the grumpy or ornery people on your staff who make your customers dread coming into your business. Fire those people today and hire someone with an amazing smile, lots of energy, and a sunnier out-look on life. You'll pay the same for that kind of person, and they can dramatically improve your customer service.

If you run a brick-and-mortar business, I don't have to tell you that online shopping has taken a big bite out of your sales. Most people who shop in person nowadays do so because they want to take something home that day. They're trying to scratch an itch that online shopping can't scratch for them, which means you have a huge opportunity.

When that customer walks through your door, you should treat them to an experience that makes them forget about online shopping. To do that, you need knowledgeable employees in place who possess the confidence to close a deal.

Employees have to be knowledgeable because customers are coming to your business having already done their research online. A whole new layer of pressure gets added when the customer comes in knowing as much or more than the salesperson. The first sign of perceived incompetence is enough for some people to walk out the door.

Your employees will never know *everything* about what they're selling, but you have to equip them with the knowledge they need to be experts. If your business isn't converting leads into customers, look to see if customer service is the problem. You might need new buyer scripts or a different set of expectations for employee-customer interaction. If your approach is sound, add new training to reinforce employee expectations.

I would bet that the adjustment you need to make relates to communication, especially if you're a larger organization. When success depends on multiple lines of communication, there are more opportunities for things to fall apart along the way.

If your numbers aren't telling a story you like, examine your communication first.

## THE INTANGIBLE VALUE OF ADJUSTMENTS

Much of the value you get from making adjustments doesn't show up on a spreadsheet. You can't quantify the peace of mind that comes when you know the challenges you're facing. As a business owner, I feel secure when I confront a problem and put a plan in place to deal with it. Even if my adjustment doesn't produce the desired results, I learn from that experience and move forward better equipped to try again.

Good habits develop when you persist with a numbers-based, logical approach to making adjustments in your business. Emotions are easily swayed, so by training your mind to deal with stressful situations in a way that removes emotion from the equation, your business can remain steady and avoid euphoric highs and crushing lows.

Adjustments also create a story the same way your numbers do. When you hit a rough patch and self-doubt starts to creep in, you can look back at your numbers and see that you've been through stretches like this before and you made adjustments that helped you bounce back. A dose of perspective is all you need to restore your confidence.

Making adjustments in your business shifts you from a pessimistic to an optimistic mind-set, and when success is 80 percent psychology, that shift has a profound impact.

Creating a strategy based on looking at your numbers allows you to take control of your business. I've already mentioned that our company's stretch goal for 2016 is to do a billion dollars in sales. The realistic number we wanted to hit was $800 million, but like we talked about in chapter 3, you can't be afraid to dream a little bigger. Right now, we'll hit $800 million, but we're behind on our stretch goal.

If I responded to every challenge with emotion, I'd be throwing my hands in the air and waving the white flag of surrender. But I know that making adjustments based on the numbers has put our company in a place where a billion-dollar year is possible.

So, here's what I'm going to do: I'm going to speak to our office leaders to formulate a strategy and then get our agents focused on making tiny adjustments that will push us well past $800 million. We might look at improving efficiency, communicating better, or reaching more contacts every day. These small 2 to 3 percent adjustments in multiple areas have the power to increase our revenue 30 to 40 percent because of the compound effect.

Adjustments based on numbers are the reason we went from zero to a billion dollars in sales faster than any real estate office in the country within the past five years.

Another secret to our success? We never attach ourselves to a particular outcome. Let's explore why your business should look at multiple measures of success.

# DON'T BE ATTACHED TO THE OUTCOME

* * * * * *

Have you ever lost $75,000 worth of business in one day? I have.

What started out as a day with so much promise quickly became a nightmare scenario that I never could have imagined. I had eight deals lined up to close and, one by one, they started falling through. Each cancellation twisted the knife in my gut a little deeper until, by about the sixth or seventh one, I was too numb to feel anything.

By day's end, all eight deals had fallen apart, and I had lost about $75,000.

For a twenty-five-year-old agent just getting started in the real estate world, this was a massive blow. My coach at the time had taught me not to be attached to the outcome, but those words were sounding a little hollow as I stared at those canceled files.

I was trying to maintain a positive attitude, but my friends weren't helping.

"Oh my God, what are you going to do?" one of them asked, totally freaking out. The other, who was equally as shocked, said, "How is that even possible?"

My confidence was shaken, but just for a second. I thought for a moment about what options I had and realized I only had one.

"What I'm going to do," I told my friends, "is go out and get eight more deals."

On that day, I learned to commit myself to the process of achieving greatness and not define success by the end result. When you attach yourself to a certain outcome and let it alone define your happiness, you're going to be a miserable person.

Bad days like mine are going to happen. Deals are going to fall through. People are going to leave your company who you thought were in for the long haul. Bad things happen to good people and bad people alike. Misfortune doesn't play favorites.

If you are committed to following the steps we've outlined in this book, my belief is that you'll experience more highs than lows. But nobody is immune to failure.

The good news about these seven principles is that they empower you to jump right back on the horse when you get kicked off. I could have sat around licking my wounds for days after losing $75,000 in twenty-four hours, but I got right back to work.

With my faith-based mind-set restored and a clear vision of what I wanted, I made a plan to get eight more deals. I followed each step of the process and found the experience to be tremendously rewarding. Day by day, I was learning to cherish the journey and not tie my personal happiness solely to the final destination.

I enjoyed the challenge of being in a situation where I had to prove myself again. In a weird way, I was almost thankful to have lost so much, because I had a chance to come out on top, stronger than before. I looked at it as an opportunity, not a setback.

I believe that I lost those eight deals because my vision was so big. When your vision is big, you must become a bigger version of yourself to catch up to your vision. Big thinkers are unattached to the outcome, whereas small thinkers let everything bother them.

Two years after that fateful day, at twenty-eight years old, I was making $1.5 million a year in commissions. Not bad for someone whose world seemingly ended one day when eight deals fell apart and $75,000 vanished into thin air.

## WHERE SOME SEE FAILURE, OTHERS SEE OPPORTUNITY

There is a key distinction I want to make here. We spent an entire chapter exploring the importance of deciding what you want—in crystal clear detail—and then followed that up with a chapter about making a plan to achieve that goal.

Saying that you shouldn't be attached to the outcome doesn't diminish the importance of setting a goal and making a plan. It means that the end result of your efforts may not be what you had in mind, and that's OK. The end result you want may be just over the next hill, so to speak, and you have to make adjustments to get there.

The habits that are formed when you adhere to these seven principles are more of a reward than whatever outcome awaits you. Here's the cruel truth about business, and this is a fact many of you know: it's a "what have you done for me lately" world.

Our company sold 383 homes in August 2016. It was our best month ever to that point. Do you think the clients we were working with on September 1 cared one bit? Of course not! They only cared about how we could help them that day.

Every success you're going to enjoy in life is fleeting. The sun will rise the next day, people will move on, and the warm glow of victory will eventually subside. You can't get attached to the outcome, good or bad, because tomorrow presents another opportunity for you to get closer or further away from the person you want to be.

This is important, because we're not just talking about ultimate outcomes. As you're attacking your plan every day, there will be smaller outcomes that could derail you if you attach undue significance to what happens.

Let's say you're on the phone with a prospect who yells at you to never call them again and hangs up the phone. If you were attached to the outcome of that conversation, this one prospect's meltdown could damage your belief that you're capable of having positive phone conversations with prospects in the future.

You can't let one small outcome on one day have a giant ripple effect on your future. In this case, you chalk it up to a conversation that didn't go your way and let it go. Maybe the prospect was having a bad day or just really hates talking on the phone. Whatever it was, that conversation is over and should not impact your aspirations.

This truth applies even as you enjoy more success and those daily outcomes involve larger dollar amounts and carry larger ramifications. I'll give you a recent example from my own life. A few weeks ago, I had a key employee in our company resign after being with us for four years. On top of that, I lost $48,000 on an investment.

A double whammy like that would throw some people for a loop. The news didn't faze me one bit. Sure, I'll miss that employee and my $48,000. I didn't want them both out of my life in the same week. But I've been at this long enough to know that setbacks are par for the course whenever you're working to build something amazing. Setbacks should be used as data points, not triggers for emotional breakdowns.

The way I see it, unfavorable outcomes are God's way of testing you to see how serious you are about working hard to achieve greatness. As you know, I'm dead serious about my personal growth and the growth of our company. So, what did I do?

The day of the resignation, I instructed our HR department to put out several ads. The next day I had three interviews with potential hires. After those were over, I started looking for new investments to recoup my losses.

When setbacks slap you in the face, some people love to cry, "What am I supposed to do now?" My response is: "What else am I supposed to do but move forward?" Attaching myself to those two outcomes would've only caused suffering.

I preferred to dust myself off and get back to work.

## EVEN POSITIVE OUTCOMES HAVE DRAWBACKS

The one lesson from Tony Robbins that transformed how I respond to setbacks and deal with failure was this: you can either live in a beautiful state or a suffering state.

A beautiful state is fueled by gratitude. When I lost $48,000 on my investment, I could've been angry, bitter, or depressed. Instead, I was grateful to be in a position where I could invest that kind of money in the first place. When my key employee resigned, I could've given him the cold shoulder or talked about him behind his back. Because I live in a beautiful state, I chose to be grateful that I got to work with him for four years.

A suffering state is not going to serve you nor will it change the situation. You won't feel better by indulging in negative feelings like fear, stress, anger, entitlement, sadness, envy, or frustration. In fact, you're going to feel much, much worse.

Choosing to live in a beautiful state makes you feel positive, powerful, and secure in your future. Can you see how that outlook helps with handling setbacks?

As we've discussed already, business is 80 percent psychology. A suffering state causes you to doubt yourself, act with zero conviction, and expect a negative outcome at every turn. If you see a business that appears capable of growth but isn't growing, I can almost guarantee their decision makers are stuck in a suffering state.

Businesses that operate with that mind-set can't get out of their own way. When they hit a bump in the road, everything unravels. By not learning how to handle setbacks, suffering businesses are setting themselves up for failure down the road.

Suffering is a snowball rolling downhill—the more you feed it, the more unstoppable it becomes. The only way to escape suffering is to live in a beautiful state and not attach yourself to the outcome. Only then can you respond to failure with gratitude.

I'm not just talking about negative outcomes here. Positive results have drawbacks, too.

Our company sold 289 homes in March 2016 and celebrated, then our sales fell off a cliff the following months. Adrian got a taste of success at his store and stopped working to attract new customers. We stop moving forward when we achieve something great.

The problem is that if you're not moving forward, you're moving backward. There's no standing still in business, as Adrian and our agents can both attest. A positive outcome should serve as nothing more than affirmation that you're on the right track. When we treat it like the finish line, we get in trouble.

Whether the results be good, bad, or neutral, you have to keep attacking your plan every day with what I like to call *patient impatience*. What I mean is that you must be patient with your day-to-day process because results won't happen overnight. At the same time, you have to go after what you want with an intensity and a desire that says you want it to happen right now.

When you're patiently impatient, you've got your head down, you're moving forward, and you're getting results sooner than you think, because you're not looking for them.

Whatever the results, put your head back down and keep moving forward. I don't care if you just made a million dollars. What are you going to do to make two million?

## TAKING THE LONG VIEW

I've spent years in business finding my resolve and refining my approach to handling the ups and downs. I have the benefit of perspective that allows me to take the long view when things go sideways in my personal life or business.

But what if you're a young professional just starting out? How do you handle success and failure when a lack of experience makes every new moment feel monumental?

I wish there were an easy answer, but the truth is you need an extra dose of resilience when you're jumping into this crazy world we call business. Setbacks can only derail you if you're not expecting them, so my advice would be to expect lots of setbacks.

For those moments of real struggle and self-doubt, let's bring back our favorite exercise: Future You! Dust off your time machine and let's journey into the future once more.

I want you to look ten to twenty years down the road and envision the person you want to become. Picture yourself sitting at a gorgeous wooden desk running a company you built with your own two hands. You can see your Mercedes parked outside when you look out the windows of your corner office. Just beyond your office door is the steady hum of activity that tells you today is shaping up to be another profitable day for your company.

Can you see that version of yourself in your mind's eye? The trappings of success might look different depending on your tastes, but Future You is definitely living the good life.

Let's look past the surface level now and go inside the mind of the you that's sitting at that fancy desk. How did you get to where you are at that point in the future? What's your work ethic like and what kind of mind-set do you possess?

As you think about the personal qualities that fueled your rise up the corporate ladder, consider Future You's decision making in particular. When faced with the situation you're in right now, what choice would they make? What if you made that same choice today?

I was channeling my future self when I reacted to losing eight deals by saying I'd find eight new ones. When I was sitting in that cramped bedroom with a busted AC unit and two kids cooling off in an ice chest, I saw a future where that wasn't the reality for my family. Future Me would've gotten off his butt and gotten to work, so that's what I did.

Future You is popular with corporate leaders—they call it future-casting—when they're trying to plot their company's future. You can use it to gain perspective when you're still learning the ropes of your industry and dealing with highs and lows you've never experienced before.

I used this strategy with a coaching client of mine named Robert whose goal was to be the top salesman in his company in 2015. Three months into the year, he hadn't closed a single deal. He came to me struggling to find meaning in ninety days of failure. I was proud of him for that because some people would've simply quit.

The first thing I asked Robert was what he wanted. When he told me he wanted to be the top salesman in his company, I wanted to know if he had the fortitude to reach that goal after his terrible start that year, or if he wanted to throw in the towel and quit. He was adamant about staying the course and accomplishing his goal for that year.

You know the next step we took—creating a plan to get Robert what he wanted. After that, we created an accountability system that included Robert tracking his numbers so we could study them together and make adjustments. Our meeting fired him up so much that when I turned him loose with the plan, he took MIA.

Throughout it all, I coached him to make sure he wasn't attached to any specific outcome. He realized he had an uphill battle ahead of him, but he was committed to it.

Robert ended up doing double the business in 2015 that he did in 2014 and earned double the income. He's also one of the top salesmen in his company now.

Three months in 2015 could've stopped that from happening. Robert chose to take the long view, and it completely changed his life. When I say you shouldn't attach yourself to outcomes, I don't say it haphazardly. I say it because I've witnessed countless times what can happen when you cherish the process and stop worrying about the results.

### WHEN IN DOUBT, START AT THE BEGINNING

I designed this book as a roadmap you could consult any time you felt adrift in life or in business. This was never intended to be something you read once and tuck away on a shelf. The lessons we've covered are real, applicable, and actionable.

I've been in business since I was a teenager, and I still adhere to these seven principles all these years later. So many people want to flip a switch and become an instant millionaire. It doesn't work that way. I'm living proof of the fact that a formula for success exists, but it requires resiliency and an unwavering commitment to your vision.

There's a reason the seventh and final principle involves the outcome of your efforts. When you don't attach yourself to results and you're constantly moving forward, you'll always be working through the process outlined in this book.

Step seven isn't at the opposite end of the spectrum from step one. They're right next to each other in the circular system that I've put together.

If you find yourself frustrated or aren't seeing the results you want, are you placing too much value on the outcome you've built up in your head? What would happen if you broke away from your original version of success and envisioned something different?

Better yet, what if you added value to the world with no preconceived notions of how you would benefit? Instead, you waited to see how value would be added back to your life.

I heard a story once of a kid named Tyler who was trying to land a summer job. He filled out applications at dozens of restaurants and stores and nobody hired him. One night he was sitting around the dinner table with his parents dejectedly talking to them about his inability to find a job even though he was ready and willing to work.

"Where would you like to work?" his father asked.

Tyler thought about it for a second and replied, "That new clothing store in the mall. A bunch of cute girls work there, so if nothing else, I might get a date out of it."

"If you want to work there, do something to show them that they'd be crazy not to hire you," his father told him. Tyler thought about his father's words, and with the next day being Saturday, he decided to drop by the store and see how inspiration would strike.

When he arrived, he saw the store was messy. Clothes were unfolded and scattered across the displays. There were tags and other trash strewn across the floor. The cute girls Tyler wanted to work with were sitting behind the counter, absentmindedly chatting with each other. As he surveyed the scene, Tyler saw his opportunity.

He began folding clothes and putting the displays back in order. With the girls watching in confused silence, he asked for a broom so he could sweep the floors. The girls got him a broom from the supply closet and Tyler swept up all the trash. By the time he was done, the store looked immaculate. The girls had bemused smiles on their faces.

"I'll see you all tomorrow," Tyler announced. The girls waved to him as he left.

Tyler showed back up on Sunday and went through his routine from the day before. As he folded shirts and swept the floor, the manager walked out from the back and watched him intently. He approached Tyler as he scooped up the last bit of trash from the floor.

"Son, can I ask why you're doing all this?" the manager said.

"I'd like to work here," Tyler told him. "I wanted to show you why you should hire me."

The manager, impressed with Tyler's gumption, hired him on the spot.

Tyler made a plan and took MIA. He put himself out there with no guarantee that his efforts would land him a job. I tell that story to illustrate the value in not attaching yourself to the outcome. Things won't always turn out the way you hope. Tyler could've gone into that store and had the manager tell him to buzz off. Even if he hadn't landed the job, would it have been worth it if he landed a date with one of the girls who worked there? I think Tyler would say his efforts were still worthwhile!

The roadmap we've laid out in this book has no beginning or end. You can hop in when you feel lost and find what you need. If you work each of these steps with an unrelenting passion and keep an open mind about what will happen, you will achieve your dreams.

Those dreams just might look different from what you imagined.

# CONCLUSION

## LESSONS TO REMEMBER

We've been on quite a journey in this book! Starting with my humble beginnings in a rough Los Angeles neighborhood, we then explored the seven principles of resiliency that developed during the years I've spent navigating the highs and lows of business.

These principles are practical, not theoretical. Each chapter is packed with applications you can use if you need help getting your life or business back on track.

As we close out our journey together, I want to give you some lasting takeaways from each of the seven principles we've covered in this book.

## LIVE BY FAITH, NOT FEAR

This principle lays the foundation for everything that follows. I want you to remember that you have a choice. No matter what the world tells you, or what your ego might whisper in your ear, you ultimately decide how to live your life. You can live by faith and embrace the power of possibility, or you can live by fear and never attempt anything amazing.

Our inside world creates our outside world. Until you create a world in your head that can reflect the outside world you want, you're powerless. No plan or inspired action or adjustments can remedy that problem. You have to start with your mind-set.

Once you take that step, your destiny is in your hands.

## DECIDE WHAT YOU WANT

If you're not crystal clear about what you want, you're not going to get it.

The best way to decide what you want from life is to look ten years into the future and envision your ideal life in seven categories: family, mind-set/beliefs, business, contribution, fitness, income, and wealth creation/personal finance.

From this exercise will emerge your heart's deepest desire, the lighthouse atop the cliff that will keep you moving forward during life's storms. Your desire doesn't have to be financial in nature. The seven principles apply whether you're talking about getting in shape for a marathon or opening your own business—or both!

Decide what you want and write it down. Talk about it with your spouse, your friends, or your business partner as often as they're willing to listen. Dreams seem more achievable and less scary when you say them out loud, so spread the word whenever you can.

The only way you can hit a target is when there's actually a target to hit.

## MAKE A PLAN

Before you ever put together your plan, you need to take your goal and stretch it. Make it bigger than you think you could ever achieve. Think about how many business owners you've heard say, "Our business has grown beyond our wildest dreams!"

You should write out a new plan at the beginning of each year. I think most people are scared to do that because they overthink what a plan should include. Keep it simple:

- What are some numbers you want to achieve?
- What's the schedule you need to follow to get those numbers?
- What are some targets you can set up to make sure you're on track?
- Who in your life is going to hold you accountable?

Boom, there's your business plan. Your plan will grow and evolve once your numbers start coming in, but you can keep it simple starting out. The point of your plan is not to figure out the magic formula, but rather to get you moving forward.

### TAKE MASSIVE, INSPIRED ACTION

Let's break down MIA into its three components. *Massive* means huge, life-changing action. *Inspired* is the feeling you should have every morning when you think about working through your plan. *Action* is what you need to take every day. Remember: if you're not moving forward—taking action—you're moving backward.

MIA is the engine behind your dreams. You have to work hard on a daily basis and let your plan and your vision drive that action. Eliminate from your mind the idea that you're going to arrive some day and get to stop working. Every successful person will tell you that they work just as hard, if not harder, now that they've achieved some of their goals. A taste of victory fuels them to soar even higher.

You're going to have to be resilient and persevere through challenging times. But at the end of the day, if you keep taking massive, inspired, faith-filled action every day, nothing can stop you from creating the world you want for yourself.

## TRACK YOUR NUMBERS

Pilots can't fly planes without their instrument panels. Can you really expect to lead your business if you aren't tracking your numbers? Without numbers, you're flying blind.

Your numbers will tell you the story of your business. I've worked with people who didn't track their numbers or didn't consult them because they were afraid of what they'd find. This mentality never made sense to me. If you're on a sinking ship, that boat is going down whether you choose to accept it or not. By refusing to consider your numbers, you are dooming your business to fail or, best-case scenario, putting a cap on its growth.

Your business personality type might prevent you from tracking like you should. If you're a skilled producer like me, you need to either hire someone to manage your business or step outside your comfort zone to do it yourself. The numbers you track should measure not only how much money you're making, but where your money is being spent.

Don't get lazy when success comes and stop tracking your numbers. That's the quickest way to halt your forward momentum and get sent back to square one.

### MAKE ADJUSTMENTS BASED ON THE NUMBERS

Tracking your numbers is not enough. To continue our pilot metaphor, if the gauges tell you the plane is headed for a mountain, wouldn't you adjust course to avoid crashing?

Of course you would. Running a business is no different: you must have the discipline to look at your numbers once or twice a day and diagnose problems when they arise. The issue could be related to training, communication, or motivation. As you check off the boxes, you'll move closer to finding the real problem and fixing it.

You must always remember that business is 80 percent psychology and 20 percent strategy.

Any issue that arises will involve some kind of internal factor. That doesn't mean every problem requires a psychological remedy, but psychology will play some role in your solution. The mind-set chapter came first in this book because your thinking informs your actions.

You'll receive peace of mind when you make adjustments based on your numbers. Even if the adjustment you make doesn't fix the issue, you can take comfort knowing that you're in control of what happens, plus you're one step closer to the right answer. Plug away until you find the right solution, and you'll be back on track in no time.

## DON'T BE ATTACHED TO THE OUTCOME

No victory lasts forever. Whatever outcome you have in mind is not the finish line, and if you treat it as such, your happiness will be short-lived. The persistent pursuit of that goal and the habits you're forming are the ultimate reward of these seven principles.

Bad outcomes don't necessarily equate to failure. Sometimes you need to rewrite your definition of success or realize that what you want is just within reach if you're resilient enough to keep pushing forward. Again, your mind-set makes the difference.

Are you choosing to live in a beautiful state or a suffering state?

On the flip side, successful outcomes are rife with their own unique pitfalls. A positive result is merely another data point that lets you know you're on the right track and can proceed full steam ahead in the direction you're going. If you get lazy and stop doing the things that made you successful in the first place, you're asking for trouble.

The resiliency roadmap is a circular process that you should be working through at all times. When you feel lost, jump back into this book and you'll find what you need.

### A FINAL CALL TO ACTION

My mission in life is to help people grow, so I hope this book has done that for you.

As you move forward in your journey, I would ask you to bring people alongside you who need to learn these seven principles. Share this book with them, and then stand beside them as they work to change their mind-set, develop a plan, and go after it. A tough journey is always more manageable when you have accountability partners.

If you'd like to be part of an ongoing discussion of things we covered in this book—and much more—subscribe to *The Danny Morel Show* on iTunes or Stitcher, or watch us on YouTube.com/DannyMorel.

We've got about 40,000 downloads per month right now, and momentum is on our side. I say at the top of every show that I want to impact your life with the actionable insights we deliver each week, I know your life and business can be enhanced if you'll join us weekly.

We have amazing guests talking on topics like mastering your morning routine, tripling your business, getting your spouse onboard with your vision, the mental side of selling, and a great deal more.

You can connect with me on Facebook (facebook.com/ Danny.Morel.Page) and on Twitter and Instagram (@ DannyMorel). You can visit my website for updates (www. DannyMorel.com). I would love to hear how this book has helped you or any topics you'd like to see me cover in my next book.

I am deeply committed to helping you succeed in any way, shape, or form that I can.

Now go out there and *be more*, *do more*, and *expect to HAVE more!*

# ABOUT THE AUTHOR

**DANNY MOREL** is a business and sales coach and the founder of Intero Real Estate Services of Southern California, one of the area's fastest growing real estate companies. He founded Intero with the goal of restoring the relationship between a broker and an agent by providing an environment where agents were properly coached, trained, and held accountable. By tackling issues like low energy and a lack of focus, Danny has helped agents increase their productivity anywhere from 30% all the way up to 4,000%.

Named as one of the country's top 50 influential Hispanics by Hispanic Business and twice named an Inc. 500 CEO,

Danny has dedicated his career to changing the lives of those who work with him. He impacts lives beyond Intero through *The Danny Morel Show*, a podcast he started in 2016 that is already one of the 125 most popular career podcasts on iTunes. When he's not working to improve the lives of others, Danny enjoys spending time with his beautiful wife Claudia and their three boys. You can follow him on Facebook (facebook.com/Danny.Morel.Page) and on Instagram and Twitter @DannyMorel.

# YOU CAN BE MORE, DO MORE, AND HAVE MORE.

I want to help you.

Every week our podcast does an incredible job at reminding you what's possible, and I look forward to answering your questions live on the show. Visit www.dannymorel.com to subscribe.

While you're there, join the community for free and receive training and updates to help you achieve more.

**WWW.DANNYMOREL.COM**